LOVE & POETRY

TAYLOR SWIFT

Published in 2025
by Gemini Gift Books
Part of Gemini Books Group

Based in Woodbridge and London

Marine House, Tide Mill Way,
Woodbridge, Suffolk IP12 1AP
United Kingdom

www.geminibooks.com

ISBN 978-1-78675-173-7

A CIP catalogue record for this book is available from the British Library.

Manufacturer's EU Representative: Eurolink Compliance Limited, 25 Herbert Place, Dublin, D02 AY86, Republic of Ireland. admin@eurolink-europe.ie

Printed in China

10 9 8 7 6 5 4 3 2 1

CAROLINE YOUNG

LOVE & POETRY

TAYLOR SWIFT

CONTENTS

INTRODUCTION

A car is travelling along a country road in upstate New York, winding through sun-speckled woodland where the leaves are blazing red and gold. The driver of the car, a bearded man in his 20s, dressed in flannels, can't stop looking over at the girl in the passenger seat, whose hair is the colour of the autumn leaves. She smiles back at him, and as she squeezes his hand tightly, she feels overwhelmingly besotted in this new relationship.

This scene is from the 2021 short film that accompanied the ten-minute extended version of Taylor Swift's 'All Too Well'. The video brought to life the "plaid-shirt days" so clearly conveyed in the lyrics of this song, particularly in its opening scenes. As the girl follows him into his family's house and soaks up these new surroundings that offer a hopeful glimpse of the future, she unwinds the red scarf from around her neck and hangs it on the banister. For every Taylor Swift fan, this moment was everything.

Since her debut album in 2006, Taylor's lyrics have become a puzzle to solve – none more so than in 'All Too Well', which, by the time of the release of the short film, was firmly part of her lore.

The original song, from the 2012 album *Red* was never a single, but it was a clear fan favourite for its perfectly crafted lyrics that chimed with all those who had felt the excruciating pain of the end of a relationship. The power was in the lines that conveyed so much in their succinctness, from the joy of nighttime kitchen dancing to the pain of breakup phone calls.

By the time of the release of *Red*, her fourth album, it had become an enjoyably addictive game to guess what – and who – her songs were about. While she didn't name names, she left clues like cake crumbs in the liner notes for each album, hinting at the famous men who had broken her heart. And for 'All too Well', the hidden

PREVIOUS SPREAD Taylor at the Grammys, 2025.
OPPOSITE Taylor cheering on her boyfriend, football player Travis Kelce, and his team the Kansas City Chiefs at an AFC Championship NFL football game in Baltimore, 2024.

message within the song lyrics in *Red*'s album sleeve referred to maple lattes.

In the autumn of 2010, celebrity gossip magazines were splashed with candid photos of Taylor walking the streets of Brooklyn with actor Jake Gyllenhaal on Thanksgiving. She had one arm draped around his puffer-jacket-clad shoulders, the other holding a Starbucks cup, and a striped scarf wrapped around her neck. They were both in joyful, loved-up mode, laughing at each other's jokes and seemingly unaware that they were in the sight of photographers. In other photos, taken on the same day, Taylor was walking and chatting with Jake's sister, Maggie Gyllenhaal.

All these clues – the festive latte, the scarf, the visit to his sister's house – clearly linked her relationship with Jake to the lyrics in 'All Too Well'. The folkloric scarf is used as a device to frame the journey of the relationship, from being left at his sister's house, as homely as the blissful peak of a romance, to being kept in a drawer as a memento of regret. Maggie was even quizzed in interviews as to whether she really did have it. But the scarf wasn't as literal as it had been interpreted. Taylor later revealed that the red scarf was a metaphor for the loss of virginity and the breaking of first love.

As she recounted to *Rolling Stone* in 2020, she was in the studio with her band, nursing the pain of her recent breakup, when she crafted the lyrics. She was so mad and emotionally drained, feeling like "a broken human", that she scrawled out words on paper until she'd created a ten-minute song. Afterwards, she called up songwriter Liz Rose to help her edit it down to a standard length for the album. Despite not being a single, it took on a life of its own, credited as a piece of genius songwriting, with *Rolling Stone* in 2021 naming it one of the 500 greatest songs of all time.

Like the aesthetics of her short film, Taylor Swift is often considered cosy and comforting. She's pumpkin spice lattes and autumn leaves, she adores cats, she wears her heart on her sleeve and she writes about love. As a teen country music star, she forged an "adorkable" persona, the nerdy girl who is pining for the cute guy, and in an early bio, as featured on her website, she described her favourite thing as "writing about life, specifically the parts of life concerning love. Because, as far as I'm concerned, love is absolutely everything".

This tendency to sing about heartbreak and idealized love in fizzy pop songs and country ballads led to her being nicknamed "the queen of the breakup song", and her appeal to teenage girls meant she was often dismissed as frivolous and non-serious – not a "proper" musician. Even as she was breaking records and winning awards, she was ridiculed for writing about her real-life relationships – never mind that's what The Rolling Stones and Bob Dylan were doing in the '60s. It's the classic double standard for a female artist, whose life – and love life – is scrutinized endlessly. Throughout her career, she has railed against the sexism that has touched her from the earliest moments in her stardom, describing how she was so often "slut-shamed" for being "man hungry", while at the same time being called a prude for not wishing to strip off for sexy photoshoots.

What is undoubtedly evident, and what those with internalized misogyny have often failed to appreciate, is the sheer breadth of her talent. Taylor is a poet and wordsmith who can fire off a hit record in an instant, where she tunes in to her own emotions to capture universal feelings. Her music wouldn't have been so immensely popular, and she wouldn't have won 12 Grammys and 40 American Music Awards, if that were not the case.

Her songwriting has been compared with that of Joni Mitchell and Bob Dylan, her lyrics on a par with the poetry of William Wordsworth (who she referenced in the beautifully haunting 'The Lakes'). Her songs resonate with all those who have felt like outsiders, like they don't fit

"Writing about life, specifically the parts of life concerning love... as far as I'm concerned, love is absolutely everything"

TAYLOR SWIFT

OPPOSITE An early publicity photo of Taylor Swift as a teen country music star, Nashville, Tennessee, 2006.

OPPOSITE The infamous VMA incident: Kanye West jumps onstage after Taylor Swift won the 'Best Female Video' award during the 2009 MTV Video Music Awards at Radio City Music Hall in New York City, 2009.

into society's neat boxes, and even though she is singing about her own experiences, they are relatable to people of all ages. There's a Taylor song for every mood: funny, upbeat, catchy Taylor ('Shake It Off', 'We Are Never Ever Getting Back Together' – often the first release from an album); heartbreaking Taylor ('All Too Well', 'I Almost Do', 'White Horse'); the Taylor who makes you catch your throat when she sings of loss and life's cruelty ('Ronan', 'Soon You'll Get Better', 'Bigger than the Whole Sky'); infectious Taylor, with synthy pop that you can't stop playing ('I Knew You Were Trouble', 'Cruel Summer'); the carnal ('False God', 'Dress'); and the vengeful Taylor, where she helps you express your own desire for revenge ('Picture to Burn', 'Karma', 'Mad Woman').

From being the youngest artist signed by the Sony/ATV publishing house at the age of 13, to having sold an estimated 114 million albums worldwide, she has been a consistent force of talent driven by ambition and hard work. As a young country star, she followed the tradition of country music in always embracing her audience, connecting with them on MySpace and on her website – an Internet baby using the new tools to forge a community – and treating them as friends, rather than just fans, as they grew into a behemoth of "Swifties".

She was all too aware that in the fickle music business she needed to keep changing, as young female musicians were considered replaceable (as reflected in 'Nothing New'). She infused country with soft rock and dubstep elements into *Red*, then shifted into an '80s synth sound with *1989*, an album that dominated the pop charts and launched her as a pop cultural icon. There was her darker, revenge-laden *Reputation* and the softer, colour-infused *Lover*. Then there were her lockdown cottagecore albums. During the global pandemic, she released *Evermore* and *Folklore* and gained a whole new audience who enjoyed the folk sound and collaborations with musicians like Bon Iver.

Yet there have also been controversial moments and challenges by provocateurs who have sought to undermine her, and moments in her career when she felt like she was imploding from the intense social media trolling. "I've been raised up and down the flagpole of public opinion so many times in the last 20 years. I've been given a tiara, then had it taken away," she told *Time* in 2023.

At the MTV Video Music Awards in 2009, as she was collecting her award for Best Female Video for 'You Belong with Me', Kanye West stormed the stage, grabbed the

ABOVE Taylor Swift in 2010, around the time of the release of her third album, *Speak Now*.
OPPOSITE Exchanging friendship bracelets with a young fan during The Eras Tour.

microphone, and declared her an unworthy winner. She was a relative newcomer, just 19, and she looked stunned and upset at the intrusion. It was a moment that would have a lasting impact on her career, but she refused to be intimidated when she continually faced up against powerful figures like West, his then-wife Kim Kardashian, and record executive Scooter Braun.

When her original record label, Big Machine, sold her first six records to Braun without her knowledge, she at first felt powerless not to have control of her own music. But then, in a groundbreaking, monumental move, she decided to rerecord each one. She released them with bonus songs "from the Vault" to give listeners a reward for playing Taylor's new version rather than the original. The result? Some of the rerecorded versions were an even bigger success than the originals. It proved to be a way of regaining control of her music and taking revenge on those who "stripped me of my life's work".

Taylor is a billion-dollar businesswoman who has become the saviour of the music industry, or, as Bloomberg boldly claimed in 2014, "Taylor Swift *Is* the Music Industry." She's the top-played artist on Spotify and Apple Music, and she is the highest-grossing female performer of all time. She is her own CEO and one of the savviest marketers, with a complete awareness of how to promote herself as a brand on social media.

On the release of *1989*, she was a trailblazer in trademarking the catchiest phrases from her lyrics to protect them from unauthorized merchandising. When she released *Midnights*, her tenth studio album, in

LEFT Performing at the 43rd Annual CMA Awards in 2009. **OPPOSITE** Looking every bit the model in a Union Jack-themed outfit, performing at the Victoria's Secret Fashion Show, 2013.

October 2022, she further rewarded fans by issuing collectible vinyl with different colour themes, special editions with bonus tracks, and coveted merchandise. In just three days she shattered modern-day sales records and sold more than one million copies. After the release of *Speak Now (Taylor's Version)* in July 2023, she became the first female artist to have four albums in the *Billboard* 200 chart's Top Ten – with *Midnights*, *Lover* and *Folklore*. She has also had more No. 1 albums on the *Billboard* 200 chart than any other woman, including Barbra Streisand.

Her astonishing success was evidenced with the sweeping grandeur of the Eras Tour, which kicked off in early 2023 and took in 60 dates in North America before travelling to South America, Asia and Europe. After seeing the Eras Tour concert in Tampa, Florida, Billy Joel compared her to the "phenomenon of Beatlemania". It was estimated that after completing 151 stadium dates in 2024, ticket sales could exceed $1.4 billion.

Despite all this, she hasn't drifted away from her fans; she's the big sister who invites them to album launches in her homes and rewards them with her "Easter eggs". These clues began in the notes on her early albums, then expanded to Instagram posts and music videos, and in the microscopic analysis of her life they help create a jigsaw of motifs and phrases that piece together significant moments.

Taylor's space is a community, a place with insider jokes and references and where friendship bracelets are worn and exchanged, just as she did at her first gigs. There is a sense of belonging here, an understanding of the frailty of human feeling and of the temporary in our connections. The emotional world that Taylor Swift has created is expressed in sheer colour – the lavender haze, the maroon of lips and bruises, the golden memories, the ocean blue of a lover's eyes and the distance between them, and the blazing red of autumn leaves, of love at its most passionate and of a scarf left behind.

1

THE EARLY YEARS

"There are videos of me walking up to strangers and singing songs from *The Lion King* when I was a baby."

TAYLOR SWIFT

OPPOSITE At the CMT (Country Music Television) Music Awards in 2006

"Hi, I'm Taylor. I love the number 13. I was born in December on a Christmas tree farm. I like imagining what life was like hundreds of years ago." These were the words that Taylor once used to introduce herself on her website. In this one sentence, she conveyed so much about her persona: the friendly approachability, the favourite number that stemmed from her date of birth and a series of "weird coincidences", her early home life where it was Christmas every day and a creative need for storytelling and expressing her emotions, which she would find in songwriting.

Taylor Alison Swift was born in West Reading, Pennsylvania, on December 13, 1989, to Andrea, who worked in marketing, and Scott, a stockbroker with Merrill Lynch. "It was such a weird place to grow up," she said in 2014 of the Christmas tree farm that they called their home. "But it has cemented in me this unnatural level of excitement about fall and then the holiday season. My friends are so sick of me talking about autumn coming. They're like, 'What are you, an elf?'"

She adored her early years on the farm, running around barefoot and helping her parents out by doing chores with her younger brother, Austin. Because she was too little to lug the trees, she was tasked with picking the praying mantis pods off the branches so they wouldn't hatch in people's homes. "It was just the most amazing, magical way to grow up," she would say of the place that fired up her imagination from an early age. She captured that enchantment in her Christmas anthem, 'Christmas Tree Farm'. The comfort of lying in her lover's arms, and of kissing under the mistletoe, transports her back to the sparkling winter wonderland of the farm. She wrote in one of her profiles on MySpace that she loves things "that make me feel seven again", harking back to that special, magical time, also conveyed in the song 'Seven'.

She had a particularly tight bond with her mother, and in 'The Best Day', one of the poignant tracks from from *Fearless*, she sings of her fond memories of being five years old, and of her doting parents and her younger brother, all of whom were supportive and loving. In 'I Bet You Think About Me', one of the "from the Vault" tracks from *Red (Taylor's Version)*, she describes her background as "humble". They were financially comfortable from her father's investment work, and their home life was warm and grounded, where their tight bond meant her parents would always nurture her creativity, without being pushy. She had known, "ever since I was born", that all she wanted to do was sing. "There are videos of me walking up to strangers and singing songs from *The Lion King* when I was a baby," she told *The Philadelphia Inquirer* in 2007.

One of the major influences in her life was her maternal grandmother, Marjorie Finlay, a celebrated opera singer whose career offered an inspiring template, and who guided the young Taylor to express herself through music. Taylor dedicated the 13th track on *Evermore* to Marjorie (with 13 being Taylor's age at the time of her grandmother's death), who she said "still visits me sometimes ... if only in my dreams." In the music video for 'Wildest Dreams', Taylor based her character, an actress, on her grandmother – sporting the same sleek dark 1950s waves in her hair, and with the cinema marquee naming her as Marjorie Finn. She told radio DJ Zane Lowe, "My mom will look at me so many times and say, 'God, you're just like her'." There was a whole mix of music in the Swift household. Her mother listened to Def Leppard when she was pregnant with Taylor, and she would continue to blast out the English rock band throughout her childhood. While Taylor was similarly devoted to them, in 'Begin Again', she describes her obsession with James Taylor, whom she was named after, and she was also drawn to female country musicians like LeAnn Rimes and Shania Twain, who were dominating country music charts. Rimes's career was a particular template for Taylor, as she was just 13 years old when she released her breakout album, *Blue*, in 1996.

In 1997, when Taylor was seven, the family moved from Pine Ridge Farm to Wyomissing, where they lived in an impressive "Georgian colonial" villa at 78 Grandview Boulevard. She enrolled at the Wyomissing Area Junior High School, but it wouldn't be a happy time. She felt awkward and chubby as she was targeted and ostracized by bullies who decided that "I was weird and they didn't like my hair".

"It was a really lonely time in my life," she added in an interview in 2007. "I was friends with a group of girls, and then I wasn't friends with them anymore, and I didn't know why. So you can translate that into really bad things in your life and let it drag you down, and do drugs or whatever, or you can find something good that lifts you above it. So I'm thankful that I found music at that time in my life."

As well as her mass of blonde curls and her height, as she towered over the other girls, what made her stick out was her single-mindedness in her desire to be a singer. At the age of ten she was given a 12-string guitar,

ABOVE Taylor Swift at twelve years old.

and she practised on it until her fingers bled. With her parents' support, she performed in Wyomissing karaoke contests and at county fairs, doing covers of the Dixie Chicks, Shania Twain, and Faith Hill. She was also given the chance to sing the national anthem at a Philadelphia 76ers baseball game in April 2002 – a great way to earn exposure in front of a huge crowd.

Once she had mastered the guitar, she began putting down words to the music. She had already been crafting poetry, winning a national contest when she was nine, so songwriting was a natural evolution. The first song she wrote, when she was 12, was an upbeat anthem called 'Lucky You', a first hint at her ability to create uplifting and catchy hooks. The second original song, 'The Outside', later featured on her debut album, was a more reflective track inspired by her own feelings of loneliness, of walking down the corridor at school not knowing who she could talk to that day. "A lot of girls thought I was weird. Actually, the word they liked to use was *annoying*. I'd sit down at their lunch table, and they'd move to a different one." She found solace in songwriting. "It's my way of coping," she says. "I write when I'm frustrated, angry or confused. I've figured out a way to filter all of that into something good." With this song, she said, "I was writing exactly what I saw. I was writing from pain."

ABOVE A young Taylor sings the US National Anthem ahead of a basketball game between the Detroit Pistons and the Philadelphia 76ers, 2002.

CMT
GIANTS
ALAN
JACKSON
133

LEFT Taylor with her brother Austin, her mum Andrea, and dad Scott in New York City, 2014.
OPPOSITE Taylor with her father, Scott, in 2008.

Rather than getting drunk at parties like her peers, she preferred to attend singer-songwriter evenings – something that made her fundamentally uncool. Feeling like an outsider would be a constant theme in her music, as she wrote of escaping the small town that stifled her, and where she used the pain as a creative tool. "The thing about being a songwriter is that no matter what happens, if you write a song about it, it's productive," she said.

The Swift family summers were spent at their second home in Stone Harbor, a wealthy Atlantic resort on the tip of New Jersey. Andrea would ask the owner of the local café, Coffee Talk, if Taylor could perform acoustic. The blonde-haired, chatty-but-serious girl would charm the customers as they sipped coffees, unaware they were hearing some of the earliest songs by a musical superstar. "My dad, my mom, and my brother come up with some of the best ideas in my career," she later reflected. "I always joke that we're a small family business." She was savvy enough at the age of 12 to snap up the taylorswift.com domain, with the foresight that she could use her website to market herself, further helping her gain traction.

Buoyed by some early success, she and her mother would go on road trips to Nashville, Tennessee, so she could hand out her demo tapes to record labels. Nashville was the home of country music, the place that burgeoning musicians with stars in their eyes could hope to be discovered. "I just got it into my head that there was this magical place that I needed to go to because that was where dreams come true," she said.

It was the place where her icons Faith Hill and LeAnn Rimes had found their sounds, and country music also allowed a creativity of expression, with raw and unflinching lyrics about love and loss. "I think all country music speaks to me," she said.

Having been shunned by her classmates, she didn't think being told no by adults would be any worse.

So, the bold 12-year-old knocked on Music Row office doors, saying, "Hi, I'm Taylor! I write songs and I think you should sign me."

The hard work paid off when, at 13, she became the youngest musician to be signed to the Sony/ATV Tree publishing house, as part of an RCA (Radio Corporation of America) development deal to nurture young artists. To make it easier to cultivate her career, the family made the permanent move to Nashville, with her dad transferring to the local office of Merrill Lynch. She was featured in Abercrombie & Fitch's "Rising Stars" national campaign as one of 27 up-and-coming young celebrities, where she was photographed with a guitar slung around her neck while dabbing imaginary tears with a tissue. Further, 'The Outside' was selected for a *Chicks with Attitude* compilation CD as a tie-in with a Maybelline beauty line and ad campaign.

Now enrolled at Hendersonville High School, much of her experience here influenced her early albums. On the first day of freshman year she sat next to the red-headed

ABOVE, LEFT Taylor enjoys an incredibly close relationship with her mum, Andrea. Pictured here at the Country Music Awards, 2010.

ABOVE, RIGHT With early songwriting mentor Liz Rose at the 2010 Grammy Awards, when their track 'White Horse' won best country song.

OPPOSITE Arriving at the Academy of Country Music Awards in 2006 in a BCBG dress and cowboy boots – her signature style.

MGM GRAND
LAS VEGAS
ACADEMY
of COUNTRY MUSIC
awards

"I didn't want to just be another girl singer."

TAYLOR SWIFT

Abigail in English class, and the two would become best friends, encouraging each other's ambitions. She still felt like an ugly duckling, but now that she was in high school, she and Abigail accepted "we were never going to be popular, so we should just stick together and have fun and not take ourselves too seriously".

She was 15 when she met Abigail, and 15 when she had her first boyfriend, and these experiences formed the basis of one of her most powerful early songs, 'Fifteen'. It captured the loneliness and confusion of teen love and dreaming of dating the boy on the football team. Yet the character in this song, as in later hits 'Mean' and 'You're on Your Own, Kid', has a greater destiny ahead of her, outside of the small-town mindset.

She found it freeing to be in Nashville, where "all of the [sic] sudden I was a normal kid", although at the end of the school day, rather than after-school clubs, she would head over to RCA to work with established Music Row songwriters. Aware that her young age might hinder her from being taken seriously, she ensured she was always prepared for her meetings, arriving armed with a handful of solid ideas. One of these writers, Liz Rose, later said that these sessions were "some of the easiest I've ever done. Basically, I was just her editor. She'd write about what happened in school that day. She had such a clear vision of what she was trying to say. And she'd come in with the most incredible hooks".

Despite the achievement of her songwriting deal, she made the difficult decision to leave RCA when she realized she might not be allowed to perform her own songs. "I didn't want to just be another girl singer. I wanted there to be something that set me apart. And I knew that had to be my writing," she said. Writing meant everything to her, and given her clear focus, leaving this big record label was a risk she was willing to take.

OPPOSITE Taylor in 2006.

2

THE DEBUT AND *FEARLESS*

> **"Her songs have these extraordinary takes on everyday life. There's a certain slant, a sense of humour and a sarcasm to them."**
>
> SCOTT BORCHETTA

OPPOSITE Taylor's original stage look brings country music to a new demographic – teenage girls.

In Nashville, the rite of passage for every musician is the Bluebird Cafe, a place where songwriters are given the opportunity to play their own songs on the same stage as established country music stars. It was where country legends Garth Brooks, Keith Urban and Faith Hill performed before they were famous, and on 4 November 2004, 14-year-old Taylor Swift took her seat on a stool on the stage. In front of a backdrop of photos of country stars, she performed a small set, including the as-yet unreleased 'Me and Britney' and 'Beautiful Eyes'.

Sitting in the audience was Scott Borchetta, a record executive who was in the process of launching his new label, Big Machine Records, and he was struck by the stage presence and songwriting talent of the teenager. He thought, "This girl has the potential to be a really big star. Her songs have these extraordinary takes on everyday life. There's a certain slant, a sense of humor and a sarcasm to them."

She became one of the label's first signings, and after sessions with producer Nathan Chapman and songwriter Liz Rose, she released her debut single, 'Tim McGraw' on 19 June 2006. It was a nostalgic ballad about the power of music and of a country song that holds a special place in a doomed relationship. Using the name of Tim McGraw, the country superstar and husband of Faith Hill, was a clever marketing tool to draw in listeners, and the song's sweet melody and lyrics earned positive reviews.

To promote this first single, she and her mother embarked on a cross-country road trip to visit radio stations in spring 2006, and she boldly offered to play acoustically for producers as a means of charming them into taking the risk of putting her on air. "I once went on the most gruelling radio tour. Living in hotel rooms, sleeping in the backs of rental cars as my mom drove to three different cities in one day," she told *Women's Health* magazine in November 2008.

Her eponymous debut album, *Taylor Swift*, was released on October 24, 2006, and she stayed on the road to further promote it to country radio. She had cowriting credits on every track, with three as the sole writer, and the tracklist included 'The Outside', one of her very first songs. It sold a modest 39,000 copies in its first week, but the momentum grew as she released further singles, 'Teardrops on My Guitar' and 'Our Song', and gained more press coverage. The album topped the country album charts and peaked at No. 5 on the US *Billboard* 200, spending 157 weeks there – the longest for any album in the 2000s. It wasn't the only record she broke. She was the first female country music artist to cowrite every track on a million-selling debut album. *The New York Times* described it as "a small masterpiece of pop-minded country".

With her glittery eyeshadow, lip-gloss smile, and sundresses worn with cowboy boots, she was marketed to a fresh demographic for country music – teenage girls. While the songs had a country bent with the peppering of pickup trucks, dirt roads and slamming screen doors throughout the lyrics, she also tapped into the confused emotions that come with being a teenager in high school. This was further buoyed by her intimate connection with her fans, both in person and online. She always took the time for meet-and-greets,

ABOVE Performing with Brad Paisley and Kellie Pickler at the 2007 Country Music Awards. Taylor had opened for Paisley's tour that summer.

to sign autographs, and later, when cell phones with cameras were ubiquitous, to do selfies.

In the mid 2000s, country music had not realized the power of the Internet, but Taylor was one of the first to take advantage of it, as she used MySpace and her website to speak to her audience directly. Most stars had a PR manager who would do the communications for them, but it was Taylor typing out her blogs, revealing a love for baking experiments, cats and the television shows *CSI* and *Law & Order* and responding directly to her fans. This all helped to make her record the best-selling country album of 2007. When she wrote on her blog that she couldn't wait to meet them in person, "whether it's in a crowd or a coffee shop", it felt completely sincere.

From these first songs, including the punchy 'Picture to Burn', there were whispers among Hendersonville's teens as to who she was singing about. While much of she wrote about at this time was observational rather than experienced, the ode to revenge on an ex-boyfriend who drove pickups he never let her drive was said to be about a boy she dated in her freshman year. Then there was the one who inspired the longing in 'Tim McGraw', her first serious boyfriend who was two years older and due to go to college. 'Our Song', a clever and upbeat ditty in which the sounds of a small southern town create the

ABOVE - Taylor Swift performs her debut single, 'Tim McGraw', in front of the star himself, at the 2007 Country Music Awards.

soundtrack to a loved-up couple, was similarly based on her very real romantic feelings, and was written for a high school talent competition.

It wasn't just boys; 'Tied Together with a Smile', was about one of her friends, "a gorgeous, popular girl in high school. Every guy wanted to be with her, every girl wanted to be her. I wrote that song the day I found out she had an eating disorder".

She conceded, "I tend to be kind of blatantly obvious, and with my songs I'll even mention names a lot of times." Although she also admitted there were "definitely a few more people who think that I've written songs about them than there actually are".

By giving her listeners such access to her inner thoughts and to her intimate relationships, she created a sense of authenticity. In the age of intense paparazzi and gossip sites, it was a clever marketing tool that came across as an uncalculated, organic decision.

Taylor was a sophomore when her debut album was released, and on the back of its huge success she switched from the classroom to being home-schooled on her tour bus. Her schedule was now packed with opportunities to perform at awards shows, as a support act for Rascal Flatts in late 2006 and for Brad Paisley over the summer of 2007.

Touring and performing was an adult world, but when she came home to Nashville, she returned to her life as a schoolgirl, where "my friends are 17. To them I'm just a 17-year-old. It's kind of interesting how you can lead a double life".

In her profile in *Time* magazine in 2023, she recounted a story of the early years starting out. She'd been booked to open for Kenny Chesney on his tour, a highly coveted spot that would be the highlight of her career. But a few weeks later she was told that because it was sponsored by a beer brand, she would be too young to be part of it. She was devastated. Later, on her 18th birthday, she received a card from Chesney, which included a cheque

LEFT Taylor Swift and Joe Jonas pictured in 2008. His sudden breakup with her inspires her to write 'Forever and Always'.

OPPOSITE Taylor in 2008. Her girl-next-door persona makes Taylor all the more relatable to her fans.

as a thoughtful gift to make up for her having to drop out of the tour. "It was for more money than I'd ever seen in my life," she said. "I was able to pay my band bonuses. I was able to pay for my tour buses. I was able to fuel my dreams."

In May 2007, she travelled to Las Vegas to perform at her first awards show, the 42nd Academy of Country Music Awards, where she performed 'Tim McGraw' in front of the man himself. She followed it in November 2007 with a performance of 'Our Song' at the Country Music Awards, where she won the Horizon Award for best newcomer. She thanked her family for taking the chance to move to Nashville, country music radio for believing in her and her fans for changing her life. "This is definitely the highlight of my senior year," she said.

Another highlight would be at the 2008 Grammy Awards, where she was nominated for Best New Artist but lost out to Amy Winehouse, who had a darker, grittier persona that was a stark contrast to Taylor's earnestness. She may have been considered a teetotalling goody-two-shoes, but the American teen didn't baulk at being a role model. She said that her point of reference in making decisions "is the 6-year-old girl in the front row of my concert. I think about what she would think if she saw me do what I was considering doing. Then I go back and I think about her mom and what her mom would think if I did that'.

If her first album had made a big impact, her second, *Fearless*, would see her fame rise even further when it was released on 11 November 2008. The title referred to the embracing of new things and not being afraid to take a risk even if you're scared. It was promoted as a major record for the 2008 holiday season, and in anticipation, Ellen DeGeneres devoted a whole episode of her daytime talk show to an album launch party.

Taylor was a perfect interviewee on shows like *Ellen*, as she had a bubbly, friendly personality. She had the looks and style, with a clear talent and passion for music, and she wasn't ashamed to speak as a real, feeling, heartbroken teenager. In the first example of her being teased for her love life, Ellen displayed a picture of Taylor with Joe Jonas on the screen. "That's ouch," Taylor responded, and she tantalizingly revealed he'd broken up with her in a 27-second phone call.

Swift's summer 2008 romance with Joe Jonas, of pop group the Jonas Brothers, was the inspiration for the track 'Forever and Always', which was written toward the very

"This song starts with this pretty melody that's easy to sing along with, then in the end… I'm basically screaming it because I'm so mad."

TAYLOR SWIFT

end of *Fearless*'s recording process. She begged Borchetta to allow her to add it to the final version of the album, as it conveyed all her confusion and heartbreak over him ending the relationship unexpectedly: "That emotion of rejection, for me, usually starts out sad and then gets mad. This song starts with this pretty melody that's easy to sing along with, then in the end ... I'm basically screaming it because I'm so mad. I'm really proud of that."

While *Taylor Swift* had led to rumours in Hendersonville as to who her songs were about, this time they would be linked to nationally recognizable names, including Jonas. 'Hey Stephen', about a "guy I had a crush on", was revealed, not so subtly in the liner notes, to be about Stephen Barker Liles of the country music duo Love and Theft, with whom she performed in 2008. She told *The New York Times* in 2008 that "every single one of the guys I've written songs about has been tracked down on MySpace by my fans. I had the opportunity to be more general on this record, but I chose not to. I like to have the last word".

Demonstrating how the ideas flowed out of her, 'Love Story', the first single from the album, was written on her bedroom floor in about 20 minutes. With its Romeo and Juliet theme, it combined her love of stories from the past and fairy-tale imagery with inspiration taken from her own life – of seeing a boyfriend every day at high school, and then, when he left for college, feeling bereft. She imagined giving Shakespeare's tragedy a twist by creating a happy ending, wondering what would happen if there was "a key change" and she turned it "into a marriage proposal".

It was followed by the single 'White Horse', which acted as the opposite of the fairy tale of 'Love Story'. This time, with the realization that there is no knight on a white horse, the romantic fantasy falls apart. The third single from *Fearless* was 'You Belong with Me', a song about a dorky teenage girl who feels invisible to the guy she is secretly pining for. This was the character Taylor most aligned with: the girl next door in the periodic table T-shirt, who is so often friend-zoned by her crush.

Taylor was now being pigeonholed as only writing about romantic love. Yet this wasn't quite true. 'The Best Day', was a tribute to her family, and in particular her mother, as a thanks for their love and support. She wrote it while touring with Brad Paisley in summer 2007, and as a surprise for Christmas that year, she played it for Andrea, with an edited home video to go alongside it. "She didn't even realize it was me singing until halfway

ABOVE Taylor's album *Fearless* scoops four awards at the 2010 Grammys.
OPPOSITE Arriving at the 2010 Grammy Awards where *Fearless* is named Album of the Year.

through the song!" Taylor said. "When she finally got it, she just started bawling her eyes out."

Its emotional heart was the nostalgia for childhood, seeing cherished memories like snapshots, and the sadness of growing up too quickly. James Reed of *The Boston Globe* named it the best song on *Fearless*. He wrote, "After an entire album of wide-open choruses, it's refreshing to hear Swift tell her story simply. If the melody doesn't stick in your mind, the message at least speaks to the heart."

Fearless was 2009's best-selling album, spending 11 weeks at No. 1 on the *Billboard* 200 and selling just over 3.2 million copies (in 2017 it would be certified Diamond, with ten million copies sold). When it was named Album of the Year at the Grammys in February 2010, she was, at that time, the youngest recipient of the award.

Taylor took to the road for her first headlining concert tour, the Fearless Tour, in April 2009, where she established her original stage look – the tumbles of curls, the sparkling fringed minidresses and boots, the drum majorette costume and the multiple friendship bracelets tied around her wrists, which she would toss out to the crowd as a way of forging an enduring connection. With 118 shows over 15 months that took her across North America and to the UK, Australia and Japan, the tour grossed $66.5 million.

Taylor had, by this point, decisively crossed over from being a country star into pop culture, and it was her unintentional role in a hugely controversial and cultural moment that had helped shift her into this new sphere. In September 2009, Taylor was due to perform at the MTV Video Music Awards, where she was also up for an award for the video for 'You Belong with Me'. Arriving with current boyfriend Taylor Lautner, star of *Twilight* (and her co-star in 2010's *Valentine's Day*), she would have no idea that what later unfolded onstage would cause ripples in her life for many years to come.

ABOVE Taylor brings the Romeo and Juliet theme to life with her performance of 'Love Story' during 2009's Fearless Tour.
OPPOSITE Taylor as a drum majorette on 2009's Fearless Tour.

3

SPEAK NOW AND *RED*

> **"I'm not going to say that I wasn't rattled by it, but I had to perform five minutes later, so I had to get back to the place where I could perform."**
> TAYLOR SWIFT

PREVIOUS SPREAD Taylor Swift's signature "heart hands" on the Speak Now Tour, Milan, Italy, March 2011.
OPPOSITE A brief moment of joy before an infamous interruption at the 2009 MTV Video Music Awards.

Standing on the stage at the MTV Video Music Awards in 2009, like a prom queen in a sparkling silver gown, this was Taylor's moment. She was the first country artist to ever win a VMA, and clutching her "moonman" trophy on the stage, she looked out over the sea of pop, R&B and hip hop acts as they cheered her. And then, when Kanye West grabbed her mic and declared, "Imma let you finish," her big moment shattered. Shocked and confused, she didn't know if the boos she could hear were for her or for Kanye, who was telling the crowd that she didn't deserve the award, but rather that Beyoncé should have won.

Backstage in her dressing room, she was in tears as her equally emotional mum tried to comfort her; it was like all those painful times at school when she was treated as an outsider and rejected by the other girls. She was shortly due to perform 'You Belong with Me', where she'd be singing on top of a taxi outside Radio City Music Hall. She pulled herself together, changed into a bright red dress, and threw her all into giving the best performance. The next day, the incident made international headline news, and President Obama even weighed in on his disapproval of Kanye's actions.

"I'm not going to say that I wasn't rattled by it, but I had to perform five minutes later, so I had to get back to the place where I could perform," she told daytime talk show *The View* as part of an extensive media debrief. Taylor felt burned, but she used the experience, as she always did, to write a song. What she created was a tender ballad called 'Innocent', which would appear on her upcoming album, *Speak Now*, and which was a gentle scolding of Kanye as a man still to grow up.

Now that she had been part of a major celebrity feud, there would be further rough patches alongside enormous success. At the Grammys in February 2010, she took home four awards, including Album of the Year for *Fearless*, but

she was also criticized for an off-key duet with Stevie Nicks that meshed 'Rhiannon' with 'You Belong with Me'. She argued against the criticism: "I write songs, and my voice is just a way to get those lyrics across."

For her third album, *Speak Now*, she would be the sole writer and co-producer for every track. The songs were once again inspired by, and reflective of, her life through 2009 and 2010. The setting of her first two albums had been high school, and now it would cover her world as a young performer, but still with the transience of relationships and the overwhelming ache of lost love. She was still the good girl of pop, with a March 2010 feature in *Elle* describing her: "The Singer – a committed teetotaler who likes to joke about her cookie-baking habit and is about to come out with her own line of greeting cards (there will be kittens, she promises, and glitter) – takes her role seriously." Asked to name the biggest mistake she'd made, the only one she could think of was forgetting to do her diary entries while rehearsing for *Saturday Night Live* (*SNL*), for which she was guest host in November 2009. But she was also game for poking fun at herself, as her self-penned monologue on *SNL* demonstrated. And at the 2008 CMT Music Awards, she performed a rap with T-Pain in which she declared herself "so gangster you can find me baking cookies at night".

ABOVE After accepting her award for Video of the Year, Beyoncé invites Taylor to deliver the acceptance speech that Kanye West prevented her from giving earlier in the evening.

The first single from the album, 'Mine', released in August 2010, was a fictionalized love story that wrapped the country pop sound around artful lyrics as she imagined herself letting her guard down in a relationship rather than running away for fear of being hurt.

The release of the album *Speak Now* followed in October 2010, instantly hitting No. 1 on the *Billboard* 200 with over one million sales. It was the fastest-selling digital album by a female artist, and it received widespread praise from critics, including *Rolling Stone*, which named it one of the 50 Best Female Albums of All Time in 2012.

The Washington Post described her as the "poet laureate of puberty", while Dolly Parton named her "the greatest thing that's ever happened to country music". She was ranked by *Forbes* as 2010's seventh biggest-earning celebrity, with an annual income of $45 million, boosted by endorsements, such as a perfume with Elizabeth Arden, advertising with CoverGirl, and ticket sales for her concerts.

The next singles from the album were 'Back to December', 'Mean', 'The Story of Us', 'Sparks Fly' and 'Ours'. They touched on the important events in her life, while not naming names (but dropping hints in her liner notes). Her autobiographical songs perfectly suited the Internet era, as sleuths pored over the lyrics to find meaning. One blogger worked out that a reference to July 9 in the

ABOVE Taylor Swift brings her famous sparkly guitar to the Fearless Tour, 2010.

song 'Last Kiss' was about her relationship with Joe Jonas, because she flew to Dallas that day in 2008 to watch him perform.

It was while filming her first movie, *Valentine's Day*, that she met Taylor Lautner, the hot young actor who had become a heartthrob with his role as werewolf Jacob in the *Twilight* franchise. They dated in autumn 2009, and she would be inspired to write the lament 'Back to December', where she referenced how he comforted her at the MTV Video Music Awards (VMAs) and how she regretted having ended it because of her own fear.

The singer John Mayer would also have a big impact on her – she had dated him when she was 19 after collaborating on his single 'Half of My Heart'. 'Dear John', with its electric guitar licks and bluesy sound, was both a heartbreaker and a revenge song that reflected the confusion she felt in the push and pull of their relationship. It painted her as a young victim, a girl in a dress crying all the way home after being unable to keep up with his ever-changing rules. It had always been a solace to express herself through music, but now her millions of fans were hanging on every word. "I feel like in my music I can be a rebel," she said. "I can say things I wouldn't say in real life. I couldn't put the sentence together the way I could put the song together."

Through the capital letter hints in her liner notes, 'Enchanted' was said to be about a fleeting meeting in New York with Adam Young of Owl City. 'Mean' was a bluegrass rebuke to the bullies who had tried to hold her back, and she also settled scores in 'Better than Revenge', reportedly about the actress Camilla Belle after she had stolen Joe Jonas from her. It was the most vicious song of her career so far. She also showed her age with the bratty 'Speak Now', where she is like a character in a rom-com who wants to break up a wedding. The transition to adulthood was a theme in 'Never Grow Up' and 'Innocent', an expression of the fear of leaving behind the safety of protected youth.

LEFT Taylor Swift met then-boyfriend Taylor Lautner while filming her first movie, *Valentine's Day*.

ABOVE The Speak Now Tour, 2011.

In February 2011, she kicked off the Speak Now World Tour in Singapore, which would finish up in Auckland, New Zealand, the following March. She was truly a global star with a devoted fan base, and during each concert she further pushed her love of codes and symbols by scrawling on her arm meaningful song lyrics by artists like U2, Tom Petty, Faith Hill, Alanis Morissette and best friend Selena Gomez.

Her most loyal fans, often wearing sundresses and cowboy boots, were rewarded at each show, when her mother, nicknamed "Mamma Swift", and an assistant would venture into the audience and select the lucky ones to invite backstage. Taylor did not want the VIP meet-and-greets to be simply for those who paid enough money; rather, they were for those who knew all the words and had spent hours making their signs.

In 'Never Grow Up', she sings about the sad transition from childhood to adulthood, of being desperate to leave home, but once in her own apartment in a big city, it's a lonely, colder place. It was an experience she had gone through, having recently moved out of home and into her own luxury condo in midtown Nashville in 2009. It was the same building she had once pointed out to her mother because "it just looked so grown-up". The huge windows provided a direct view of Music Row, the strip of recording studios and label offices that is a beacon to all ambitious musicians. She decorated her apartment in a whimsical style, which she described as "Tim Burton-*Alice in Wonderland*-pirate ship-*Peter Pan*". There was a Juliet-style balcony overlooking the living room, which featured a koi pond, antique gilded birdcages, a giant human-sized birdcage housing a chill-out room, such kitsch treasures as a topiary rabbit in a marching-band hat, framed photos of her family and friends and a framed picture of the moment when Kanye crashed her acceptance speech, to which she had added the handwritten note: "Life is full of little interruptions."

It was in this Nashville apartment, and while on tour, that she had begun composing music for what would be a first transition towards a new sound. With the sense that she needed to evolve, she was adamant she wanted to move towards pop-rock for her fourth album, *Red*.

Swedish pop magicians Max Martin and Johan "Shellback" Schuster worked with her on three songs: 'We Are Never Ever Getting Back Together', 'I Knew You Were Trouble' and '22'. They still possessed the classic Swift narrative, the clever phrasing, the heartbreak and joy,

Dunlop
Gibson
Les Paul

but they shifted away from her original country sound of banjos, fiddles and mandolins in favour of electric guitars and even a dubstep bass-drop. She had begun her career as a teenager with a Tennessee drawl, but she allowed it to soften. Taylor's look of sparkling dresses, boots and a mass of curls would also change as she cut and straightened her hair, chose leather shorts and blouses and bowler hats, and made red lips her signature.

'We Are Never Ever Getting Back Together', released in August 2012 as the first single from the album, was pure pop. In the studio with Martin and Shellback one day, she expressed her frustration at a relationship where they were continually on and off again, and the Swedes encouraged her to develop it as a catchy song. On release it was dismissed by some critics as frivolous, but it was a crossover hit, dominating country radio and pop charts around the world.

The upbeat song was supported by an equally fun music video, where she danced in pyjamas and glasses in her bedroom while supported by her band dressed as fluffy creatures. In reality, she had the blonde looks of a cheerleader, but so often in her songs and videos she was the underdog. Throughout *Red,* she took aim at the hipsters – the guy whose indie records are cooler than hers, those who sneer "ew" at the mention of her name in '22', and the "Not a lot going on at the moment" T-shirt worn with red heart-shaped glasses in the music video. She was poking fun at, and self-aware of, her own uncoolness at the same time. It may have been laced with the joyousness of a 22-year-old who was "single and happy and carefree and confused and didn't care", but the album came from a place of deep sadness, where she had spent the last Christmas crying over "this earth-shattering... absolute crash-and-burn heartbreak", thought to be caused by the older actor Jake Gyllenhaal.

The only way she could heal was to express it in songwriting, and red, she said, was the colour she immediately associated with fast, out-of-control love and loss, which, in the title track, was like a Maserati speeding down a dead-end street. She also used the motif to good effect in 'All Too Well', a song about her autumn relationship with Gyllenhaal, whose presence was felt throughout the album.

In a world of raunchiness, Taylor was considered prim and straitlaced – more akin to a princess in a fairy tale than a modern, scantily clad pop star. For the first time, she hinted in *Red* that she was not the good girl

"Red was the colour Taylor immediately associated with fast, out-of-control love and loss."

OPPOSITE Performing and turning on the Christmas Lights at Westfield Shepherd's Bush, London, 2012.

ABOVE Jake Gyllenhaal at the Academy Awards, Los Angeles, 2010.

people thought she was. On 'Treacherous', written with Dan Wilson, she breathes, "I'll do anything you say if you say it with your hands." In 'Girl at Home', she resists being the other woman in a cheating man's life. And in 'I Knew You Were Trouble', which was a dubstep risk for her, the guy in the song takes her to places she's never been. The extended video, where she plays a hipster girl abandoned at a music festival by the bad boy, won the Best Female Video award at the VMAs in 2013. She said in her acceptance speech: "I also want to thank the person who inspired this song, who knows exactly who he is." While it had originally been written about someone else, it was now a missile directed at Harry Styles, who she dated at the end of 2012. At the Grammys the following month, her performance of 'We Are Never Ever Getting Back Together' further appeared to reference him, when she put on an English accent for the interlude.

Having made $57 million in 2012, she was one of the best-selling female recording artists in music history and had a tireless work ethic, as well as "an Oprah-like gift for emotional expressiveness", according to *The New Yorker*, yet she was reduced to being a serial dater. She was incredibly frustrated that her love life was a joke,

ABOVE Taylor performing at the 2012 iHeartRadio Music Festival at the MGM Grand Garden Arena in Las Vegas in September 2012.

even when she made her own digs at her penchant for revenge ("So what are you going to do? Did you not Wikipedia me before you called me up?").

At the November 2012 Country Music Association Awards, hosts Carrie Underwood and Brad Paisley made fun of her short-lived romance with Conor Kennedy, which is believed to have inspired 'Begin Again', a ballad about a reviving new love. "Are they ever gonna get back together?" Paisley asked. "Like never," replied Carrie. "Maybe she'll write a song about it," added Brad.

There were similar jokes at the 2013 Golden Globes by the hosts Tina Fey and Amy Poehler, where she was nominated for Best Original Song for 'Safe and Sound' from *The Hunger Games* soundtrack. Taylor was in the ladies' room at the time, but the auditorium laughed at her expense. She later told *Vanity Fair* that she admired Katie Couric for saying, "There's a special place in hell for women who don't help other women."

Following the release of *Red*, she was now the first female artist – and the fourth artist ever – to have two albums (after *Speak Now*) sell a million copies in their first week. She was also the first female artist to have three consecutive albums hit No. 1 on the *Billboard* 200 for six weeks or more. She embarked on the Red Tour in March 2013, which further demonstrated she was a true crowd-pleasing star. As much as it was a heartbreak album, of eviscerating pain and anger at having her trust damaged, it was a celebration of her youth. Tracks from the album lent a power to her arena performances, with 'State of Grace' as a dramatic, soaring opener. Each concert also had a uniform aesthetic that tied in with the album's mood, with her red lips, high-waisted black shorts, white shirt and Oxford brogues.

She may not have been the best dancer, but, as *The Guardian* commented in its review of the show at London's O2, she was "most at home when she's behind an instrument" and demonstrating her true "songcraft".

Even as she was promoting *Red*, she was thinking of her next move, as she confessed that as soon as she put out one album she was "already worried about the next one". And her fifth album would take her to a whole new level of fame.

OPPOSITE Taylor accepts her awards from Daft Punk and Pharrell Williams at the 2013 MTV Video Music Awards in August 2013.

4

1989

> "I was really putting my neck on the line, because I was the one saying I need to change directions musically."
>
> TAYLOR SWIFT

While bringing the Red Tour to venues around the world, Taylor was continually collecting thoughts for her fifth album – recording voice memos, noting down lyrics, and playing with ideas for the direction she wanted to take. After *Red* lost out on Album of the Year at the Grammys in 2014, she chose to go for a completely new sound – and to signpost this rebirth, it would be influenced and named after the year she was born. It was also inspired by her transformational move to New York City. "It's so big and bright," she told *Cosmopolitan* in 2014. "I needed a new challenge and there's no bigger challenge than uprooting your life, finding new places to hang out, new friendship circles ..."

She teamed up again with Max Martin and Shellback, as well as collaborating with producer Jack Antonoff, to fully shift from country to pop by way of 1980s synths and programmed drums. She had already experimented with the dubstep on 'I Knew You Were Trouble', and given that it had spent seven weeks at No. 1, the risk had paid off. She was also inspired by new friends in her embracing of '80s pop. "I was with Jack Antonoff and Lena Dunham at the beach, and we started talking about our favourite '80s music. All of this started happening organically, and I found myself gravitating toward pop sensibilities, pop hooks, pop production styles," she said.

Her record label, Big Machine, tried to persuade her not to make a straight-up pop record, strongly suggesting she still include a couple of country songs with their fiddles and banjos. Even calling the album *1989* and using a Polaroid image for the cover that only featured half her face was considered a gamble, but she was adamant. "I was really putting my neck on the line, because I was the one saying I need to change directions musically. And my label and management were the ones saying, 'Are you sure, are you positive? This is risky.'"

PREVIOUS SPREAD Taylor Swift performs at the O2 in London in 2014. **OPPOSITE** Taylor snapped in Manhattan on 14 November 2014.

LEFT Taylor Swift performs during her 1989 Secret Session with iHeartRadio on 27 October 2014 in New York City.

OPPOSITE Performing at Dick Clark's New Year's Rockin' Eve, in Times Square on 31 December 2014.

The first single, 'Shake It Off', released in August 2014, was an infectious number taking aim at the trolls. The pure pop sound, with its cheerleading beat, went straight to No. 1 on the *Billboard* Hot 100, and it would earn three Grammy nominations. With her savviness in ensuring her own words were not exploited, its catchy phrases were some of the first song lyrics to be trademarked.

The accompanying video depicted her as the nerdy girl struggling to keep up with different forms of dancing, yet it also showcased a new look – the sleek blonde bob and a more streamlined New York style that would punctuate the next few years.

As well as its familiar themes of love and heartbreak, the album was a celebration of living in New York. She had been terrified of this change, but once she overcame the fear, she experienced the thrill of being in a city that inspired so many other artists, as expressed in the feel-good opening track of the album, 'Welcome to New York', which extolled all the possibilities of life in the beating heart of a thriving, liberated city.

In an interview with *Rolling Stone* in September 2014, she confessed to being single and loving it, and after a series of bad relationships she now wanted to focus on herself. It was during this incarnation that she embraced new famous friendships and lived the lifestyle akin to that celebrated in her ode to having a good time, '22'. If her last album was about the "deep, sad, intense heartbreak I went through", then this album was "after that, when you've figured it out. You like being alone and not because you're hurt, not because you're sad, but because it's free'.

"I really like my life right now," she said. "I have friends around me all the time. I've started painting more. I've been working out a lot. I've started to really take pride in being strong. I love the album I made. I love that I moved to New York. So in terms of being happy, I've never been closer to that."

She may have celebrated being young and free and embracing the heartache with mascara tears in 'New Romantics', yet the ghost of her relationship with Harry Styles was present throughout the album, particularly on the tracks 'Style' and 'Out of the Woods'. She was the girl with the red lips and tight little skirt, and he was the boy in the T-shirt and slicked-back hair who got into a snowmobile accident and ended up in a hospital room. In 'Wildest Dreams', she goes further than before when it comes to forbidden love – remembering his hands in her hair and his clothes in her room.

The album was a celebration of a woman finding herself after a reckless romance, and this was expressed in 'Clean', the final and 13th track. Together with 'Shake It Off', it was one of the last songs she wrote for the album, conceived when she was in London. Walking out of Liberty department store, she was struck by the realization that someone she used to date had been in the same city for the past two weeks, and she hadn't thought about him at all. She felt that she was finally clean and ready to move on, and the secret message in the liner notes was "she lost him but she found herself and somehow that was everything".

Taylor had long felt stung by the misperception of who she was, as played up in the press and in jokes by comedians. So she chose to embrace the role of a serial dater in the satirical 'Blank Space', where she acted as the seductive but crazy girlfriend. "That was the character I

felt the media had written for me, and for a long time I felt hurt by it. I took it personally. But as time went by, I realized it was kind of hilarious."

'All You Had to Do Was Stay' was inspired by a dream where her ex came to her door and begged her to take him back, and all that she was able to respond with was a high-pitched call to stay. "I woke up from the dream, saying the weird part into my phone, figuring I had to include it in something because it was just too strange not to. In pop, it's fun to play around with little weird noises like that."

> "I am in love with catchy melodies and hooks that are stuck in your head for days, and ideally weeks, and even months."
> TAYLOR SWIFT

Above all, she wanted the songs on the album to be addictive. "I am in love with catchy melodies and hooks that are stuck in your head for days, and ideally weeks, and even months," she told *Time* magazine.

Her instincts about the album were right – when *1989* dropped in October 2014, it sold 1.28 million copies in its first week, more than any album in that time period since 2002, and it topped the *Billboard* 200 for 11 non-consecutive weeks, spending the next year in the Top Ten. It also received strong reviews: *Time* praised the songs that "fizz and crackle with electricity and self-aware wit", while *Pitchfork* described a grown-up Swift who was now inhabiting "a fully-realized fantasy of self-reliance, confidence, and ensuing pleasure".

In a novel exercise in reaching out to her fans, Taylor scoured Tumblr and fan blogs to select a chosen few to come to her homes for "Secret Sessions", where they got the chance to meet her parents and to try out her home baking while hearing a preview of the album before anyone else. As part of the deluxe edition, she also let listeners in on her creative process by including memos and voicemails to her producer with ideas for her songs. It was a deliberate rebuttal to the misogynistic assumption that she was not the creative force behind her own work. Given that Ed Sheeran was never questioned as to whether he wrote his own songs, she said, "We all know it's a feminist issue."

Rolling Stone described *1989* as "The Reinvention of Taylor Swift," and *Time* splashed her on the cover of the 24 November 2014 edition with the headline, "The Power of Taylor Swift." In December, at the *Billboard* Women in Music event, she accepted the title of Woman of the Year, making her the first artist to win the award twice.

It was the most successful album of her career so far, and with this powerful position, she now had

ABOVE, LEFT Channelling a more streamlined New York style that punctuates the next few years.
ABOVE, RIGHT Hanging out with Karlie Kloss, in New York City, 2014.
BELOW Lorde, Selena Gomez, Taylor and Karlie Kloss at the 2014 American Music Awards on 23 November 2014 in Los Angeles.

confidence in standing up to the music streamers that exploited artists. She had long felt that artists' work was devalued by Spotify, and in November 2014 she took a stand and removed her entire back catalogue. When Apple announced a three-month trial for its subscription service, during which time artists would not be compensated, she was so angered that she penned an open letter. She wrote, "We don't ask you for free iPhones. Please don't ask us to provide you with our music for no compensation." By the end of the day, Apple had reversed the decision, and she was hailed as the saviour of struggling musicians.

With the previous pressure she had experienced on her love life, her break from dating was a way of trying to stamp out the accusations that she was a serial dater. Instead, her apartment in New York became a gathering place for her celebrity girlfriends, known collectively as the "squad". This included Lena Dunham, singers Lorde and Selena Gomez, and top supermodels Karlie Kloss, Cara Delevingne, Kendall Jenner and Lily Aldridge.

The Tribeca townhouse, previously owned by *Lord of the Rings* director Peter Jackson, was almost as whimsical as her Nashville penthouse, but was rich and dark, with leather and wood and velvet. It made appearances on Instagram as she recorded her life with her BFFs and with her cats, Meredith Grey, inspired by *Grey's Anatomy*, and Olivia Benson, after the Mariska Hargitay character in *Law & Order: Special Victims Unit*. Karlie Kloss regularly stayed over in her own guest bedroom, and Taylor had a rack full of white nightgowns so that she and another close friend, Lena Dunham, could dress up as "pioneer women, fresh off the Oregon Trail".

Having turned 25 in December 2014, she had truly transitioned from the lanky 15-year-old who had dreamed of escaping high school. Now she was living in luxury in the hippest city in the world, with some of the most beautiful, coolest women as best friends. Her millions of followers on Instagram could watch her getting ready for the Met Gala with Kloss or baking cookies with Hailee Steinfeld.

As a September 2015 *Vanity Fair* profile described, she "lunches and dines with these girlfriends; she attends concerts with them; she crafts with them; she cooks with them; she walks red carpets with them; many of them appear

OPPOSITE The 1989 tour in 2015.

in pre-taped clips that run during her current world-tour stops; and some of them have even emerged, in the flesh, at her shows, to strut down the stage and wave to the crowd".

When she performed at the Victoria's Secret show in London in December 2014, she looked every inch the glossy-limbed supermodel – a marked change from the geeky girl in glasses who used to dance on her bed. She now had her own clique that she had not only been accepted into but was de facto leader of. Years later, in the track 'You're on Your Own, Kid' from her *Midnights* album, she referenced the pressure she felt during this *1989* period. She overexercised and starved her body to be as thin as she could be, and felt she had to live up to always being the perfect host of parties, to the detriment of her own mental health.

It was as if she was enacting revenge on the girls who rejected her when she was at school. It was the same reason she had purchased a silver Lexus SC 430 convertible after her first flush of success, as it was the one driven by Regina George in the 2004 movie *Mean Girls*, a character the girls in Pennsylvania idolized.

ABOVE Singing with Mick Jagger in 2013. Taylor's performances with other famous faces often invited accusations of name-dropping.

OPPOSITE Looking like a glossy-limbed supermodel, Taylor Swift takes to the runway for the Victoria's Secret Fashion Show at Earl's Court on 2 December 2014 in London.

But there was speculation on social media and in comment pieces as to whether Taylor had turned into a "mean girl" herself, particularly with the release of the music video for 'Bad Blood', where she had recruited her famous friends to play girl power assassins. It won Video of the Year and Best Collaboration at the 2015 MTV Video Music Awards, but the song was a barbed attack on another woman. She strongly hinted in an interview with *Rolling Stone* that it was about her feud with Katy Perry, who allegedly poached Taylor's dancers from one of her tours.

In May 2015, she embarked on the 1989 World Tour, which crossed North America, took in dates in Europe, Asia and Australia, and grossed over $250.7 million. On each stop, she would invite a special guest to perform with her, such as Jennifer Lopez, The Weeknd, Ellie Goulding, Mick Jagger and even members of her squad, further leading to criticism that she was a name-dropper.

When *1989* won Album of the Year at the 2016 Grammys, Taylor became the first woman to win this top award twice. It was a glorifying moment as she was photographed with a blonde bob and an armful of awards, but now that she was at the peak of her career, there was destined to be a backlash. During her acceptance speech, she made an obvious dig at Kanye West: "I want to say to all the young women out there, there are going to be people along the way who will try to undercut your success, or take credit for your accomplishments, or your fame."

Having reunited at the 2015 Grammy Awards, it appeared as if Taylor and Kanye had made peace. The two were close enough to go for dinner in New York, to chat over phone calls, and she hinted that she'd be open to a collaboration. But then, at the beginning of 2016, in his new track, 'Famous', he claimed credit for her success and called her a "bitch". She had become one of the most significant performers of the 2010s, selling over one million albums in a week for her last three albums, all the while receiving warm reviews from critics.

LEFT Taylor Swift hugs Kanye West after presenting him with the Vanguard Award at the 2015 MTV Video Music Awards in Los Angeles, California.

OPPOSITE, ABOVE At the 2016 Grammys, Taylor accepts an armful of awards, becoming the first woman to win Album of the Year twice.

> "I want to say to all the young women out there, there are going to be people along the way who will try to undercut your success, or take credit for your accomplishments, or your fame."
>
> TAYLOR SWIFT

It was galling that someone would use misogynistic lyrics to undermine her achievements.

There would also be another celebrity feud over the summer of 2016. Taylor had avoided dating for the past few years, but in March 2015 she began a relationship with Scottish DJ Calvin Harris. They were first seen holding hands at a Kenny Chesney concert in Nashville, and they began showing up in each other's Instagram feeds, cavorting in LA swimming pools and celebrating the Fourth of July together.

When they split in June 2016, Taylor announced that she had in fact cowritten his hit collaboration with Rihanna, 'This Is What You Came For', under the pseudonym Nils Sjöberg. Harris lashed out at her revelation. The world Taylor had created around herself, and her reputation, was about to implode.

LEFT With Calvin Harris at the 2015 *Billboard* Music Awards in Las Vegas in May 2015.

5

REPUTATION

"I pushed away most people in my life because I didn't trust anyone anymore. I went down really, really hard."
TAYLOR SWIFT

On 29 August 2016, Taylor wrote in her diary, "This summer is the apocalypse." Her '80s-infused album *1989* had stormed the charts, earning critical acclaim and an armful of Grammy awards, and so it was inevitable that there would be a backlash. "I had all the hyenas climb on and take their shots," she later reflected, and these shots felt like continuous bombardment.

There had been too much publicity – following her split with Calvin Harris, she began a very visible relationship with actor Tom Hiddleston after meeting him at the Met Gala in May 2016. As co-chair of the fashion event, she was the star of the evening, rocking an edgier goth look with a silver snakeskin minidress, bleached hair and black lips to suit the theme: "Manus x Machina: Fashion in an Age of Technology." She had invited the rock band Haim, who were close friends, to perform, and a video emerged of her and Hiddleston doing a dance-off, at a time when she was still supposedly dating Calvin Harris.

Two weeks after she officially called it quits with Harris, paparazzi photos captured Taylor and Hiddleston kissing on the rocks near her Rhode Island home, and it was splashed on the front page of *The Sun*, with the headline "Tinker Taylor Snogs a Spy" (referring to his role in the John le Carré television adaptation *The Night Manager*).

Quickly dubbed "Hiddleswift", they travelled around the world on her private jet and were snapped holding hands at the Colosseum in Rome. During Fourth of July celebrations with her new best friends Blake Lively and Ryan Reynolds, the actor was pictured frolicking in the waves in an "I heart TS" T-shirt. If people needed a reason to believe Taylor was eager to move on to another relationship, then this was the evidence, and all the perfect photo-ops seemed too convenient, like they were a massive PR stunt.

PREVIOUS SPREAD On the Reputation Tour in May 2018. **OPPOSITE** "Hiddleswift". Taylor enjoys a short-lived but very visible relationship with actor Tom Hiddleston in 2016.

That summer, the fallout with Kanye West came to a head following the rapper's release of a disturbing music video for 'Famous', in which a nude waxwork in Taylor's likeness was in bed with Kanye, his wife Kim Kardashian, Donald Trump and other celebrities. In July, Kardashian posted on her Snapchat account the recording of a phone call between Taylor and Kanye, where it appeared she had in fact consented to the reference to her in 'Famous'. It painted Taylor as a liar who had played the victim.

On 17 July, World Snake Day, Kim further twisted the knife when she tweeted: "They have holidays for everybody, I mean everything these days," and her fans headed straight to Taylor's Instagram, where they bombarded her with snake emojis.

Taylor released a statement over the leaked call, stating she would "very much like to be excluded from this narrative" – words that would come back to haunt her. With #taylorswiftisoverparty trending on Twitter, and gossip blogs and magazines speculating on her cancellation, she retreated completely from public view. "Literally millions of people were telling me to disappear. So I disappeared. In many senses."

After her split from Hiddleston, she had quietly begun dating the British actor Joe Alwyn, and as she divided her time between New York and his hometown of London, she ensured she kept the relationship completely private.

"You have a fully manufactured frame job, in an illegally recorded phone call, which Kim Kardashian edited and then put out to say to everyone that I was a liar," she said in a 2023 interview with *Time*. "That took me down psychologically to a place I've never been before. I moved to a foreign country. I didn't leave a rental house for a year. I was afraid to get on phone calls. I pushed away most people in my life because I didn't trust anyone anymore. I went down really, really hard."

Taylor was hardly seen in public for the first half of 2017, and in August, fans were quick to notice that she had wiped all previous posts from her social media accounts. Just a few days later, she posted to Instagram a set of three videos of CGI snakes, and it was followed by the announcement that there would be a new album coming on 10 November.

Having experienced a "career death", all she could do was rise again, and this time she was taking back the power. The snake emoji had been used as a mass form of bullying, and now she was owning it as the leading motif for her new visuals.

ABOVE Showcasing an edgier look at the Met Gala, 2016.
OPPOSITE, ABOVE A rare sighting of Taylor in New York, 16 September 2016, while she tries to keep a low profile.
OPPOSITE, BELOW New beau British actor Joe Alwyn, seen here with Taylor in 2019.

The first single from the album, 'Look What You Made Me Do', was released on August 25, and it immediately set the tone. With its melodramatic strings and piano and pounding electronic drumbeats, it was an angry revenge piece that took aim at those who had attacked her. It also declared that the old Taylor was dead.

The song was about many things at once: being called a snake, her feuds with Kanye West and Katy Perry, the social media takedown. The accompanying video was loaded with references from her past to pick over. She first crawls zombie-like out of a grave marked 'Here Lies Taylor Swift's Reputation', and stands beside another headstone marked "Nils Sjöberg." Later, she is surrounded by snakes and bedecked with snake jewellery; there is a giant birdcage, like the one in her Nashville apartment; and there is a thinly veiled impression of Katy Perry with her *Witness*-era short, bleached hair, as a reference to the feud between the two.

All her previous incarnations – the Taylor with the fringed dress, boots and guitar, the one in nerdy glasses and a T-shirt scrawled with the names of her friends, and the one who says, "I would very much like to be excluded from this narrative" – are mocked and killed off by her new, deadlier identity.

As Caryn Ganz described in *The New York Times*, 'Look What You Made Me Do' was "fury, it's vengeance, it's gossip. It's a horror movie, a fairy tale contorted into a calamity … This song is for the base – the superfans on the internet who are always ready for a fight."

In one moment in the video, as she lies in a bath filled with jewels, there is a glimpse of a one-dollar bill. Over the summer of 2016, she had also been preparing her testimony for a court case against radio DJ David Mueller, who had been fired three years before when she reported him for putting his hand up her skirt while they posed for a photograph backstage. After he sued her for defamation, she countersued for just $1 in damages. When it came to court in August 2017, she was ready to fight and she refused to be bullied as she gave evidence. She won the case, and she was hailed for making an important stand against sexual harassment.

In an interview with *Time* in 2023, she described *Reputation* as "a goth-punk moment of female rage at being gaslit by an entire social structure". Although it was threaded with revealing love songs that offered insight into the crazy summer of 2016 and the romance that saved her, it was also a "complete defence mechanism". She described how isolated she had felt

during her mass public shaming and demands for her cancellation. Speaking to *Vogue* in August 2019, she said, "I don't think there are that many people who can actually understand what it's like to have millions of people hate you very loudly ... When you say someone is cancelled, it's not a TV show. It's a human being. You're sending mass amounts of messaging to this person to either shut up, disappear, or it could also be perceived as, *kill yourself*."

The album artwork was black and white, like the newspaper print that had tormented her over the last year. In the lead-up to the album's release, she avoided publicity and interviews, only sharing news and updates on social media, as a way of controlling her own narrative and allowing the music to speak for itself.

She made an exception for *Saturday Night Live*, appearing as the musical guest on 11 November, where she debuted the second single from the album, '...Ready For It?' Performing as a goth against a black background flooded with red lights and clutching a microphone wrapped with a jewelled snake, it was a swaggering, angry and suggestive performance – the most dramatic switch she had ever made in her ten-year career. *1989* had remade her as a pop star, but this new sound was

ABOVE Swifties show off their entry tickets to the civil case of Taylor Swift vs David Mueller at the Alfred A. Arraj Courthouse on 8 August 2017 in Denver, Colorado.

OPPOSITE Taylor Swift in a collaboration with Diet Coke.

jaw-dropping with its mixture of electronica, hip hop and industrial goth, exploring the dangers of stardom.

If she had made a career of feeding her fans clues through the lyrics and liner notes, then the speculation around the subject and meaning of her songs went into overdrive. As well as the Easter eggs in her music videos, each track was loaded with references as to what her life had been like over the last year. She played up to the image that had been created in the media, and rather than allowing it to consume her, she took ownership of it. In 'End Game', featuring Future and Ed Sheeran, she dips into hip hop with the chorus and raps about her big-name enemies. In '...Ready For It?' she is a schemer who plots to get the one she fantasizes about. And in 'I Did Something Bad' and 'Don't Blame Me', she plays the boys like a violin; she is the unapologetic playgirl who teases the narcissists, flies them around the world and then takes pleasure in leaving them before they can hurt her.

Similarly, in 'Getaway Car', she employs the imagery of a heist as a metaphor for her short-lived rebound romance with Tom Hiddleston – she uses him to escape a relationship and then abandons him when she doesn't need him anymore. 'This Is Why We Can't Have Nice Things' is a sneering and bratty shot at her enemies (particularly Kanye and Kim) who stabbed her in the back and tricked her on the phone. Immediately after suggesting that forgiveness might be a nice thing to do, she bursts into brittle laughter.

It wasn't all revenge and bombastic surface – there were softer tracks that gave an insight into her low-key relationship with actor Joe Alwyn, who she began dating in late 2016 after months of friendship. 'Gorgeous' imagines an instant infatuation with a guy with an accent she makes fun of and ocean-blue eyes – a recurring theme for future tracks about Joe – and she curses herself for going home to her cats instead of declaring her feelings. 'Dress' hinted at when they first met. With his buzzcut and her bleached hair, it was a clear reference to their looks at the 2016 Met Gala, and she acknowledges that he is the only one who really sees her for who she is.

The gentler tracks revealed the slow coming together of their relationship, first meeting in a dive bar on the lower east side in 'Delicate', then going back to her apartment on the west side. At a time when her reputation was at its worst, she sings that he must like her for who she really is. Yet she worries about whether she's too quick to reveal herself to him, if it's cool, or if it's too soon. In 'So It Goes',

"...a goth-punk moment of female rage at being gaslit by an entire social structure."

TAYLOR SWIFT

they also meet in a bar, and immediately wanting to be alone with him, she acknowledges she's not a bad girl but she wants to do bad things. With the lipstick on his face and scratches on his back, combined with the dress she only bought so he could take it off, the album was the most sexual of her career. She is scared in 'Dancing with Our Hands Tied' that they will be divided by the avalanche of press intrusion, and she hopes that they can get through it. She has a bad feeling, but in imagery that recalls the sinking of the *Titanic*, as the water rushes in and the lights go out, they keep dancing, ignoring the doom and prophecies.

In 'Call It What You Want', she reflects on her hibernation after her public shaming, where her castle, and her power, crumbled. The drama queens may take swings, but she feels protected by her lover, who she trusts. The final track on the album, 'New Year's Day', was a sweetly melancholic piano ballad about holding on to the memories of midnight while cleaning up the mess of bottles and glitter the next morning; being there for both the good times and the more mundane.

Reputation sold one million copies the week it was released, making it the highest-selling album of 2017.

OPPOSITE Taking back the power. The snake, previously used as a way of shaming Taylor, is a leading motif for her new stage visuals.

ABOVE Performing with a throne of snakes on the Reputation Tour.

Her song for Little Big Town, 'Better Man', won the Country Music Association award for Song of the Year, and she was featured on *Time*'s Person of the Year cover as a "silence breaker" for her victory in her sexual assault trial.

She had come back fighting, but still, she was criticized for her ambivalent stance following Donald Trump's tumultuous November 2016 defeat of Hillary Clinton. She had not endorsed either candidate, and rather than attending the Women's March in January 2017, she had only tweeted her support. How to come out politically, and how to reveal her allyship with the LGBTQ+ community, was something she would think hard about while she embarked on the Reputation Stadium Tour.

As her first all-stadium tour, it was high-tech, brash and dramatic, with pyrotechnics and video projection, but in the middle of the set, she took a break from the gothic aesthetics and snake imagery with a technicolour interlude as she performed 'Delicate'. Now wearing a rainbow-striped minidress, she spoke to the audience, their lit-up bracelets transforming them into a sparkling sea, of the value of finding something real amidst gossip and rumour. The rainbow joyousness continued with colourful confetti falling during 'Shake It Off', and following this interlude, she was back in glittering black, but this time more introspective for an acoustic performance of 'Dancing with Our Hand Tied'. Her performance of 'Dress' was dedicated to modern dance pioneer Löie Fuller, who was the openly gay toast of Paris during the Belle Époque era, and whose signature pieces included the 'Serpentine' and 'Butterfly' dances.

The Reputation Stadium Tour broke the record for the highest-grossing American tour, and for Taylor, the most emotional part "was knowing I was looking out at the faces of the people who helped me get back up. I'll never forget the ones who stuck around'. By the time she had finished the tour in Tokyo in November 2018, she was ready to find peace in new music and to finally speak out about the issues she cared about.

OPPOSITE A break from the gothic aesthetics and the snake imagery with a rainbow-hued interlude as she performs 'Shake It Off' with Charli XCX and Camila Cabello.

6

LOVER

"If there was no change, there would be no butterflies."

PREVIOUS SPREAD At the 2019 American Music Awards. **OPPOSITE** A rainbow-sequinned playsuit at the iHeartRadio Music Awards in March 2019 hints at Taylor's new direction.

If *Reputation* was a gothic revenge fantasy, where all Taylor's darkest thoughts were unleashed within its gritty black, white and red colour scheme, then her next album would be a complete about-turn.

While a clear fan favourite, *Reputation* had not been as well received as previous albums. It had sold 4.5 million copies in comparison to *1989*'s ten million and was snubbed at the Grammys. She was introspective – "I just need to make a better record" – and tonally and aesthetically, her new music would be a metamorphosis. Not only was it the first album produced under a new record deal with Universal Music Group, giving her full ownership of her works, but it was written at a time when she felt like she "could take a full deep breath again". She worked with collaborators Jack Antonoff, Annie Clark (known as St. Vincent), Joel Little, and the Dixie Chicks to hone this softer, more hopeful direction.

She would offer further clues to its mood in her wardrobe choices – arriving at the *Vogue* BAFTA party with Joe Alwyn in a powder blue wrap coat, and at the iHeartRadio Music Awards, in March 2019 in LA, in a rainbow-sequined playsuit and with heels decorated with butterflies.

The first hint that there was new music coming was an Instagram post on 13 April 2019 of a pastel background with a clock counting down to 13 days. It was followed by further teasers – including a pair of hands with pastel nails and a love heart made from diamonds.

Finally, on 26 April, she held a photo call in Nashville, where she posed against a butterfly wing mural in a powder blue skirt and top and with pink tips in her hair. She had personally commissioned the mural from street artist Kelsey Montague, and it announced the release of a new single, 'Me!', a duet with Brendon Urie from Panic! at the Disco.

This new, bubblegum-sweet single just screamed upbeat fun. There was a marching band drumbeat and a catchy chorus, and the video was laced with Easter eggs to treat her fans. It opens with a snake transforming into butterflies, a clear metaphor for the light bursting from the darkness of the *Reputation* era, and then breaks into a joyous, pastel world – as if it's the Land of Oz awakened from a curse. Taylor had revealed in an interview in 2008 that one of her favourite lines, written by a radio producer who was also a songwriter, was: "If there was no change, there would be no butterflies."

In one scene in the video, as she sits on a large unicorn gargoyle, she looks out on a cityscape with a pink neon sign saying "Lover". It would be a signpost to the name of her seventh studio album, which she announced on Instagram Live on 13 June, with a release date of 23 August, adding up to 13 (8 + 2 + 3).

She also revealed that the next single, 'You Need to Calm Down', would be released at midnight, with the music video premiering on *Good Morning America* a few days later. As a song that takes aim at Internet trolls and homophobia, it was a clear marker of her stance on LGBTQ+ rights. "The first verse is about trolls and cancel culture. The second verse is about homophobes and the people picketing outside our concerts. The third verse is about successful women being pitted against each other," she told *Vogue*.

The video was bursting with technicolour campness, as Taylor played the bikini-clad queen of a rainbow trailer park, and with cameos from queer stars, including some from *Drag Race* and *Queer Eye*. One moment saw pop star Hayley Kiyoko aim a bow and arrow at a target with the number five – a clue that the next single revealed would be 'The Archer', the album's fifth track – and Ellen DeGeneres receives a 'Cruel Summer' tattoo from Queen singer Adam Lambert, referring to the second track from the album. It ended with a call to sign a petition to support the Equality Act, which would prohibit gender- and sex-

ABOVE A powder blue coat, worn to the *Vogue* BAFTA party with Joe Alwyn in early 2019, suggests a softer, more hopeful direction for Taylor.

LEFT Butterfly heels at the iHeartRadio Music Awards in March 2019.

OPPOSITE With Brendon Urie of Panic! at the Disco fame performing their duet 'Me!' at the 2019 *Billboard* Music Awards.

> "... a love letter to love, in all of its maddening, passionate, exciting, enchanting, horrific, tragic, wonderful glory."
>
> TAYLOR SWIFT

based discrimination in the US. Taylor was now ready to bring her political stance to the fore.

She had been accused of sidestepping the important issues of the day, leading some to question what side of the political spectrum she was on. She was criticized for being silent during the presidential election, but it was exactly what she had been taught as a young female artist. The Dixie Chicks became pariahs overnight after making a stand against George Bush and the Iraq War back in 2003. Now that she had left her original label, Big Machine, after six albums, she felt more confident in being able to express her support for the issues that mattered to her. There had been hints of her pro-LGBTQ+ standing from the video for 'Mean', in which a boy wears a lavender sweater while being bullied in his high school locker room, and she previously donated to a fund for the Stonewall National Monument. But she first took an explicit stance a month before the 2018 midterms when, on Instagram, she endorsed the Democrat candidate for Tennessee and called out Marsha Blackburn, the Republican running for Senate, for her discriminatory values.

Lover would be her most optimistically romantic album so far. As she described to *Vogue*, it felt like a new beginning,

OPPOSITE Taylor showing support for the LGBTQ+ community through her wardrobe choices.

LEFT Craig Wiseman and Taylor perform onstage at Bluebird Cafe on 31 March 2018 in Nashville, Tennessee. **OPPOSITE** A live performance on ABC's *Good Morning America* on 22 August 2019 to promote *Lover*, it is also where Taylor announced her plans to rerecord her earlier albums.

and it was "really a love letter to love, in all of its maddening, passionate, exciting, enchanting, horrific, tragic, wonderful glory". Over the 18 tracks, she paid tribute to her great loves – her boyfriend and her mother, and the places that had shaped her, including New York's West Village and her new life in London.

As a way of offering a further confessional insight into her life, the deluxe editions of the album included scanned entries from the diaries she'd kept since the age of 13.

"There is an element to my fan base where we feel like we grew up together. I'll be going through something, write the album about it, and then it'll come out, and sometimes it'll just coincide with what they're going through. Kind of like they're reading my diary," she said. She also continued her tradition of holding "Secret Sessions" over the summer to give her closest fans a first listen to the album.

The upbeat opening track, 'I Forgot That You Existed', with its jaunty piano, was an announcement that she was over the *Reputation*-era feuds. She insists she's stopped thinking about the person that wronged her – she doesn't feel love or hate, just indifference, and she was truly over the pain, or was she? In 'Cruel Summer', co-produced by Jack Antonoff and St. Vincent's Annie Clark, she appeared to be writing about the painful summer of 2016, heightened by a "fever dream" new love – a blue feeling – and where its addictive bridge was the big moment of the song.

Much of the album was about her relationship with Joe Alwyn, for whom she had upped sticks and escaped to London. In the track 'London Boy', she lists all the things she loves about the city, from exploring Camden Market and Hampstead Heath, to watching rugby in the pub with his best mates from uni, including the terms "I fancy you" and "Babes, don't threaten me with a good time" lifted from her British friends. This also harks back to 'King Of My Heart' from *Reputation*, where she is similarly the American queen who he "fancies".

The dreamy 'Lover', with its stirring orchestra, was the song she was most proud of, as it idealized the ordinariness of finding a soulmate, where new rules can be created. In a *New York Times* video feature, *Diary of a Song*, she revealed the idea had come to her in the middle of the night, like a "glittery cloud" of inspiration as she imagined the last two people on a dance floor, swaying together, and wondering whether they'd known each other for 20 seconds or 20 years.

'Cornelia Street' was one of the most analysed tracks on the album, offering a tantalising glimpse into her love story. In reality, Taylor had rented an apartment on Cornelia Street, in Greenwich Village, and here, in the back of a cab after a drunken night at a bar, she offers to take someone home. She is so infatuated that she could never return to this street if their relationship were to fall apart.

There were also darker themes at play. 'The Archer' is a self-critical examination of how she makes enemies of friends, how she has been both aggressor and prey in relationships, and it expresses her anxiety around whether anyone could really stay, given how critical she is of herself.

In 'Death By A Thousand Cuts', the upbeat sound contrasts with the downbeat lyrics, where alcohol is not enough to dull the pain of a breakup, and she tries to find a part of her that wasn't touched. If 'Lover' was about all the mundane tasks of setting up an idealized home filled with romance, then in this version, the windows of the house are boarded up. 'False God' features sultry saxophones and offers a worship of the sensual as she laments the frustrations of a transatlantic relationship. The song shares the religious metaphors of 'Cornelia Street' as

well as the long-distance yearning and burn-out of tracks from other albums, including'Come Back... Be Here,' 'Hoax' and 'Maroon.'

As much as she glorified her romance, which had lasted "three summers", she would ensure the revelations were only contained within her lyrics – she was determined to retain her privacy, and so Joe was not up for discussion in interviews. "That's where the boundary is, and that's where my life has become manageable," she told *The Guardian* in August 2019.

The album wasn't all about romantic love. 'Soon You'll Get Better', a country ballad with the Dixie Chicks providing banjo, fiddles and backing vocals, revealed her mother's cancer battle and the endless stays in hospital as she tries to be optimistic about her recovery. The anthemic 'The Man' lectured on the double standards where Leonardo DiCaprio is praised for his playboy image, whereas a woman can never get away with even minor transgressions.

The final track on the album, 'Daylight', revealed her growth since *Red*, where she realizes that rather than burning red, love can be golden. It was a mature reflection on the damage over the last few years, of the cruelty of a harsh city where she became a joke and how this new love she found is an awakening.

One of the most melodramatic tracks on the album, 'Miss Americana and the Heartbreak Prince', as atmospheric as Lana Del Rey, uses a high school setting as a metaphor for how she had grown up as an unquestioning patriot, but can now see the dangers of the type of nationalism that Donald Trump was espousing.

In the documentary *Miss Americana*, which was filmed during the *Reputation* tour, she revealed how she grappled with her decision to speak up about the issues that she cared about. Her dad was worried for her safety, given the separate apartment she had to keep for her security guards and the military-grade wound coverings she carried with her due to her stalkers, but she was insistent that it was

ABOVE Taylor declares her intention to reclaim what is hers, at the American Music Awards, on 24 November 2019.

RIGHT Making history. Taylor wins six awards at the AMAs, taking her career total to 29, surpassing Michael Jackson's record of 24.

OPPOSITE Performing a career-spanning medley as the American Music Awards Artist of the Decade.

important to speak out. "I've educated myself now, and it's time to take the masking tape off my mouth, like, forever."

Lover was the top-selling album of 2019, praised by critics for its optimistic beats and a sequence that refused to stick to one sound or narrative, and it would go on to earn three Grammy nominations, including Song of the Year for the title track. At the same time as she was promoting its themes of transformational love, she was entering into a new battle with powerful figures.

Taylor had been her record label Big Machine's biggest act, but the new deals with Universal, and then Republic Records, not only gave her more agency over her own work, but a clause in her contract stated that the group would share proceeds of its Spotify equity with all its artists.

After the release of *Lover*, Scott Borchetta put Big Machine up for sale, and when Taylor asked if she could buy back the original recordings, or masters, for her previous six albums, he turned her down. She was devastated to discover her back catalogue had been sold to Scooter Braun's Ithaca Holdings as part of a $140 million deal. Braun was an ally of Kanye West, and she wondered what nefarious plans he might have for her music. She wrote on Tumblr that it was her "worst case scenario". Taylor's frankness about the painful situation of not owning her music opened a discussion around why musicians did not necessarily have rights to their own masters. She was determined to do something about it.

In August, live on *Good Morning America* as she promoted *Lover*, she announced her plan to rerecord her albums, starting in November 2020, the first point when she would be contractually able to do so. At first it seemed like an impossibly huge task, but she was driven by the outrage and anger she felt at "having my life's work taken away from me by someone who hates me".

Named as Artist of the Decade, she opened the 2019 American Music Awards standing against a black background, wearing a plain white shirt printed with the names of the six albums to which she didn't own the rights. On the back of the shirt was *Fearless*, and after opening with the pushback against mysogyny, 'The Man', she performed a medley of her greatest hits – a strong statement that she was reclaiming what was hers.

OPPOSITE Showing some girl power with Camila Cabello (L) and Halsey (R) as they perform 'Shake It Off' at the AMAs.

THE FOLK ERA

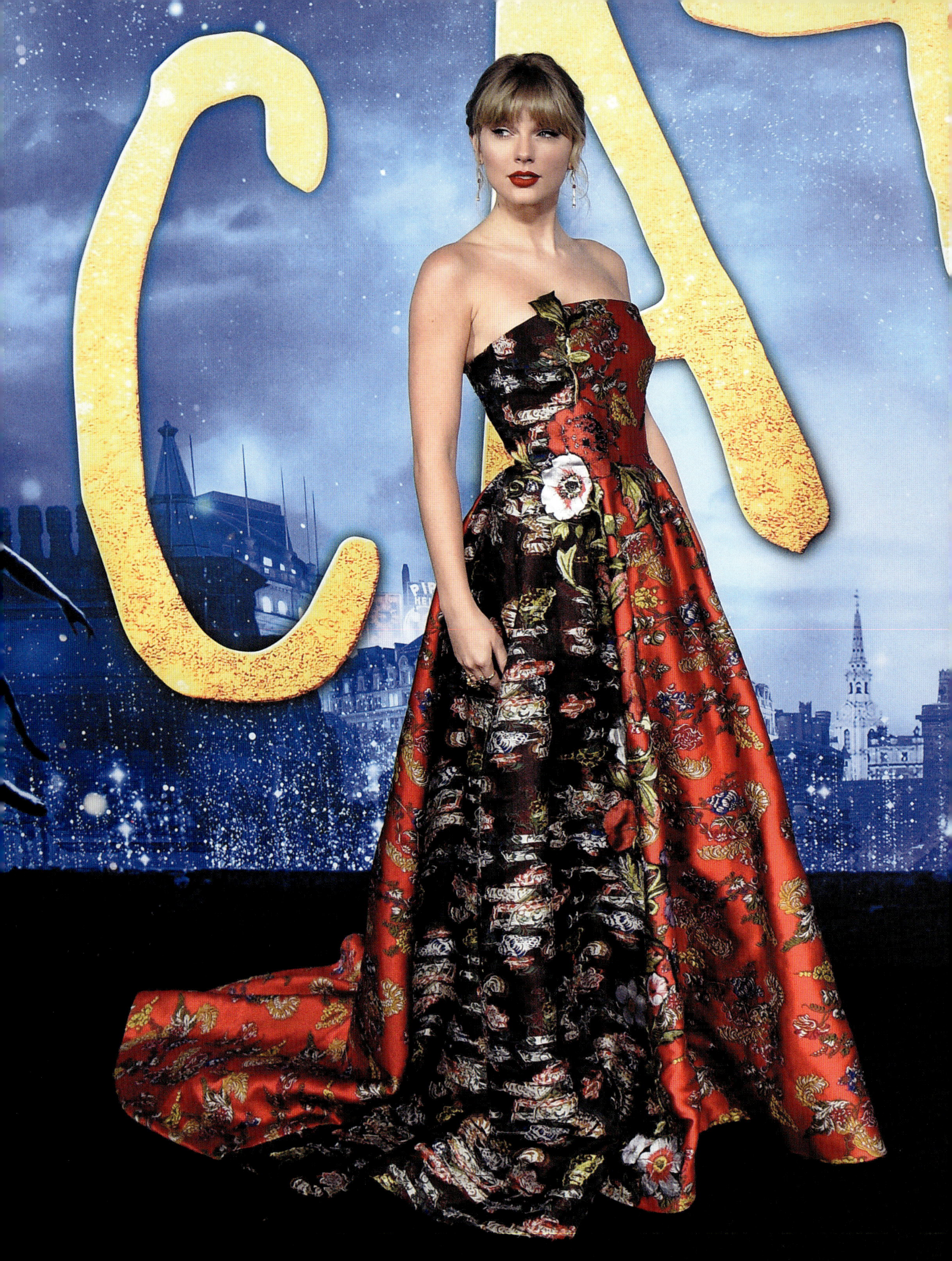

> "The lines between fantasy and reality blur and the boundaries between truth and fiction become almost indiscernible."
>
> TAYLOR SWIFT

PREVIOUS SPREAD Showcasing her folk-era style, Taylor Swift performs onstage at the 2021 Grammy Awards. **OPPOSITE** Taylor Swift at the *Cats* world premiere in New York, 16 December 2019.

In one moment in her *Miss Americana* documentary, Taylor reflects on the significance of turning 30. Now in a happier place after a tumultuous few years, she wanted to enjoy her fame and good grace while she still could, as she was well aware that female artists had a shelf life. She also thought endlessly about how her sound should evolve in this next decade.

She penned a piece for *Elle*'s April 2019 eedition – '30 Things I Learned Before Turning 30' – where she described how she learned "to stop hating every ounce of fat on my body. I worked hard to retrain my brain that a little extra weight means curves, shinier hair, and more energy", and how to make cocktails "like Pimm's cups, Aperol spritzes, Old-Fashioneds, and Mojitos because ... 2016". If she thought that year was dramatic, she would need a whole new repertoire of cocktails for 2020.

Having been excited to be cast as Bombalurina in Andrew Lloyd Webber's *Cats*, the movie bombed on its release in December 2019. Her original song 'Beautiful Ghosts', however, was nominated for a Golden Globe, and she attended the January 2020 ceremony with Joe Alwyn. Later that month, *Miss Americana* was shown at the opening night gala for the Sundance Film Festival, before being streamed on Netflix.

As for taking *Lover* on the road, she mapped out a simplified tour, with four stadium events in America, and a tour of the European festival circuit, which would have included headlining Glastonbury. Following the COVID-19 outbreak in March, and with international borders shutting down, all her dates for the year were cancelled. As stay-at-home orders were put in place, she rented a home in London with Joe and her three cats, Meredith, Olivia and Benjamin.

Taylor's lockdown was much like everyone else's who was kept at home. She cooked, drank wine on the sofa, read great novels like *Rebecca*, watched old films she'd never seen before, such as Hitchcock's *Rear Window*, and chatted to friends and family over Zoom. She also wanted to do what she could to help others who were less fortunate, and she sent money to fans who were struggling with unemployment at the time.

"I think right now we have to connect with our humanity more than we ever have before," she said during a presenting slot on SiriusXM. "So, that's one thing that I've been loving seeing is outreach, people being there for each other in this time."

On 27 April 2020, she posted an image on social media with the caption "Not a lot going on at the moment", a reference to the T-shirt worn in the '22' music video. It turned out that between Instagramming her cats, she'd been busy working on new music. With just 17 hours' notice, Taylor Swift announced a surprise quarantine album, *Folklore*.

"Most of the things I had planned this summer didn't end up happening, but there is something I hadn't planned on that DID happen," she wrote on Instagram. "I'll be releasing my entire brand new album of songs I've poured all of my whims, dreams, fears, and musings into."

She recorded the music in isolation, setting up a studio in the spare bedroom, and collaborating with her "musical heroes" remotely. These included Jack Antonoff – "basically musical family at this point" – The National's Aaron Dessner, who provided keys and piano, his brother Bryce, who developed string arrangements, Justin Vernon of Bon Iver and William Bowery, the pseudonym of Joe Alwyn.

The album came with a series of folksy black and white images by Beth Garrabrant of Taylor surrounded by forest. It not only reflected the nostalgic, alternative sound that was aligned with cottagecore aesthetics, but also of living through a pandemic, when the only way of connecting to people and the world was by going for walks in parks and woodland.

Inspired by the romantic world of poetry and storytelling, she told her audience during the *Folklore* section of the Eras Tour that the album had come from a fantasy of being in an imaginary cabin, surrounded by woodland, where she was "not a lonely millennial

OPPOSITE Sweeping in for another award nomination at the 2020 Golden Globes.

woman covered in cat hair, watching 700 hours of TV a day". Instead, she was a "woodsy Victorian lady who is wandering through the forest holding like a candlestick holder ... collecting feathers to make my own quill, to write on parchment paper. It was a whole thing".

Earning a Guinness World Record for the most opening-day streams of an album by a female artist, *Folklore* was instantly critically acclaimed, with *The Guardian* giving it five stars and *Rolling Stone* describing it as her greatest album to date. The biographical details of previous albums had been manna to her fans, but they also allowed for her to be satirized for her feuds and love affairs. This time, Taylor's songwriting took centre stage as she weaved together fictional stories. She found this freeing because it existed "on its own merit without thinking, 'Oh, people are listening to this because it tells them something that you could read in a tabloid.' It feels like a completely different experience".

The tracks were folksy, gentle and intimate – more indie than radio-friendly pop. She used the full breadth of her songwriting skills to explore fictional worlds and characters, while also developing her own universe that used reoccurring references in different tracks. As she said of the music, "The lines between fantasy and reality blur and the boundaries between truth and fiction become

ABOVE Taking selfies with fans as she arrives at the *Miss Americana* premiere, at the Sundance Film Festival, on 23 January 2020.

ABOVE *Miss Americana* was streamed on Netflix at the end of January 2020.

almost indiscernible." Given that she'd spent her lockdown absorbing literature and movies, references peppered the lyrics – from *Peter Pan* and *The Great Gatsby* in the first track on the album, 'The 1', to *Rebecca* in 'Tolerate It', and to the running metaphor of life as a movie.

There were three songs on the album, 'Cardigan', 'Betty' and 'August', that when taken together told the story of a teenage love triangle from all three characters' perspectives. In 'Cardigan', the narrator, Betty, looks back on an intense relationship from years before, where her lover, James, cheated on her. As well as being fictional, the symbolism in the song was reminiscent of 'Cornelia Street' and 'Delicate' in its exploration of a hot love affair in New York, with kissing in cars and downtown bars.

'Betty', a nod to country with its harmonica, is narrated from the perspective of James, where he reveals he ditched Betty after a school dance. As he's walking home, the other girl arrives in her car and tempts him for a summer fling. "I'm only 17, I don't know anything," he implores Betty, as he admits he screwed up. It was the fantasy that Taylor had often expressed in her songs, of a former lover returning to apologize for all his mistakes. Coming from the perspective of the other girl, 'August' reveals her infatuation during this summer affair, as she lives in hope that they could be a real couple. "August slipped away into a moment in time," and she realizes, "You weren't mine to lose."

In the sweeping 'The Last Great American Dynasty', she tells the story of eccentric heiress Rebekah Harkness, the previous owner of her Rhode Island house, and she draws parallels with her own life as the woman who shakes up this conservative community. Another biographical song, 'Epiphany', the 13th track, was about her grandfather Dean, who fought on the island of Guadalcanal in 1942.

'My Tears Ricochet', the first song she conceived for the album, and the one she considered the saddest, alludes to a devastating divorce. With its theme of karma and betrayals, she thought of the superhero stories where the hero's biggest nemesis is "the villain that used to be his best friend".

As soon as Aaron Dessner sent her an ominous piano sample, she was inspired to write 'Mad Woman', about female rage and gaslighting. While she described it as the story of a "misfit widow getting gleeful revenge", and where the reference to witches harks back to 'I Did Something Bad', it appeared to point in the direction of her real-life feuds.

Many of the tracks, Taylor said, had "lyrical parallels". In 'This Is Me Trying', the narrator, struggling in a life crisis, drives to a cliff edge to contemplate ending it all, as does the narrator of 'Hoax'. Here, the painful yearning for a lost love is like watching a film reel that was once shown in her hometown, while in 'Exile', featuring Bon Iver, as she struggles with the end of a relationship where she is now untethered from her town, she's seen the film before, but didn't like how the ending played out.

As with 'Peace', 'Invisible String' appeared to reference her relationship with Joe, using the metaphor of his love as a golden thread that pulled her away from the wrong ones, and into the blue and pink skies of her *Lover* era. The final song on the album, 'Hoax', is both a painful cry at being hurt in a relationship, as well as a reflection of having left New York, where she still feels the pain of her scars from being pulled apart. But, as she describes in 'Cardigan', he drew stars around these wounds to heal her.

There was also a bonus track, 'The Lakes', inspired by a trip to the Lake District, which is also referenced in 'Invisible String'. Just like the romantic poets who retreated there, she imagines her own escape from all the cynics who hunt her with cell phones, to a place where nature forms a secure blanket, and where she is happy as long as her muse is right beside her. This muse was Joe Alwyn, and during lockdown, as she heard him compose music on the piano, some of what he played formed part of the tracks 'Betty' and 'Exile'.

On Sunday, 22 November, she posted a black and white photo on a couch in the wooden cabin, again using the caption "not a lot going on at the moment". There was huge speculation as to what it could mean – was she about to drop a music video for 'Exile' or to announce one of her rerecords? The surprise was the release of *Folklore: The Long Pond Studio Sessions*, both as an album and an intimate concert documentary film on Disney+. In September, she and her collaborators Jack Antonoff and

LEFT Taylor performs onstage for the 63rd Annual Grammy Awards on 14 March 2021.

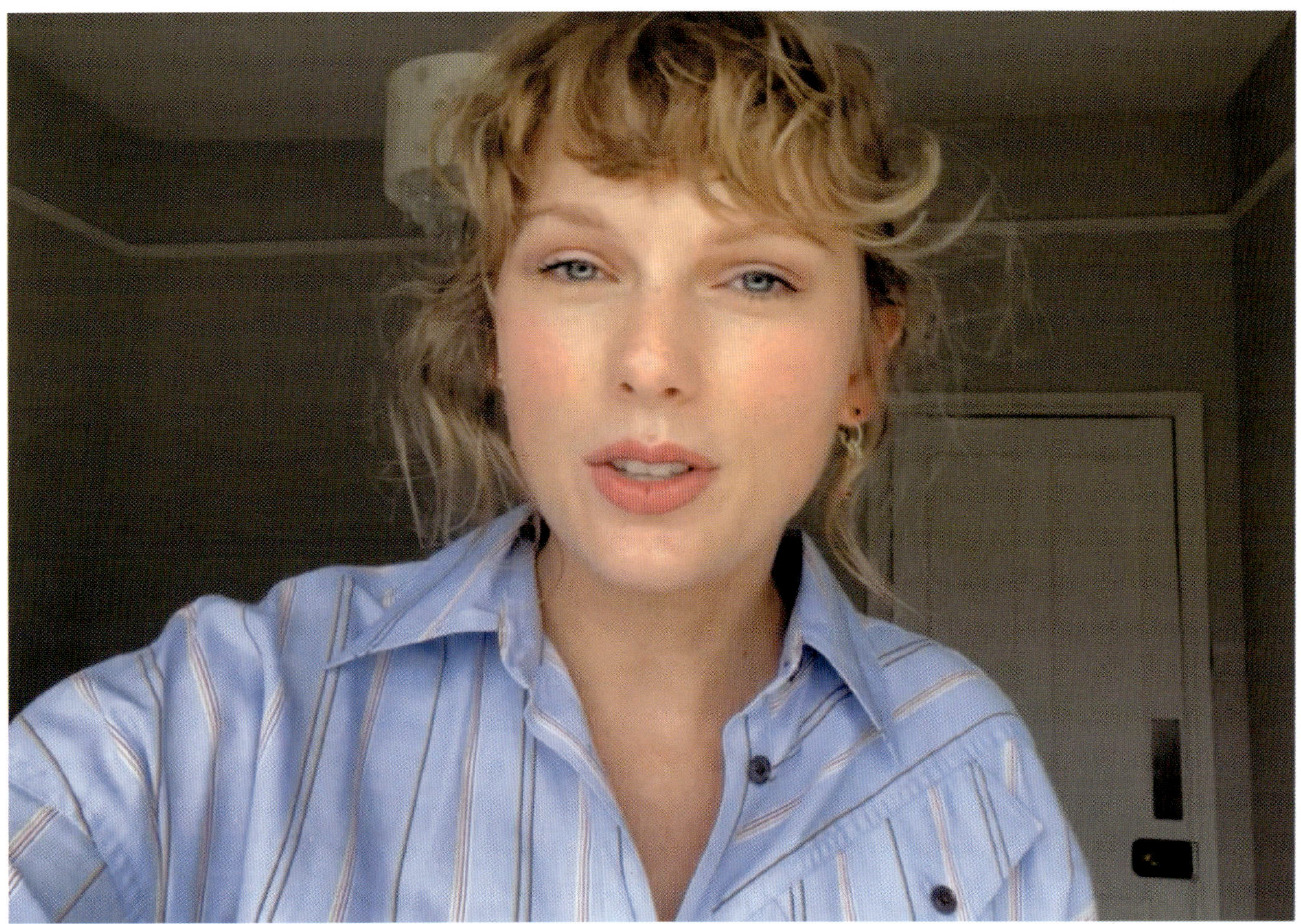

Aaron Dessner had met in person at Long Pond Studio, an isolated wood cabin in upstate New York, to record a live session of *Folklore*.

The film offered a new intimacy in seeing Taylor in such a stripped-back setting, absolutely in her element with her fellow musicians, and where the interiors of the cabin and the woodland setting reinforced the wistful sound and aesthetics. Further, it turned out that she was about to drop more music, making the announcement on 10 December that *Evermore*, the "sister album" to *Folklore*, was coming out at midnight.

"To put it plainly, we just couldn't stop writing songs," she wrote. "To try and put it more poetically, it feels like we were standing on the edge of the folklorian woods and had a choice: to turn and go back or to travel further into the forest of this music. We chose to wander deeper in."

The new cover art, which fixed on her long-plaited hair and plaid coat as she faces toward woodland, harked back to the autumnal mood of 'All Too Well'. The songs, while still folksy, were more buoyant. The picked guitars of opening track and lead single, 'Willow', set the mood for the album, and in its music video, a cardigan-clad Taylor follows a golden string into a magical kingdom, where she's a witch casting love spells in a forest.

ABOVE With the pandemic ongoing, Taylor accepted her 2020 MTV Video Music Award for her direction of the video for 'The Man', virtually.

There was a return to her country origins with 'Cowboy Like Me' and 'No Body, No Crime' with Haim, which both referred to fictional crimes. The former, featuring Marcus Mumford on backing vocals, was, as Taylor described, about "two young con artists who fall in love while hanging out at fancy resorts trying to score rich romantic beneficiaries".

'No Body, No Crime' appeared to be partnered with 'Tolerate It' as part of her self-described "'unhappily ever after' anthology of marriages gone bad that includes infidelity, ambivalent toleration, and even murder".

Another pairing was the two songs about Dorothea, "the girl who left her small town to chase down Hollywood dreams". 'Dorothea', like 'Betty', was written from a male perspective. We then hear Dorothea's point of view in ''Tis the Damn Season' as she returns home for the holidays and rekindles an old flame.

There were upbeat tracks like 'Gold Rush', where she eulogizes his ocean eyes, the golden hair falling into place like dominoes and her jealousy that others are desperate to be with him too – lines similar to that of 'Lover',

OPPOSITE At the Golden Globe Awards, The Beverly Hilton Hotel, California, 5 January 2020.

ABOVE, LEFT A surprise quarantine album, *Folklore*, is released, followed a few months later by *Folklore: The Long Pond Studio Sessions*, a live concert and documentary film about the album.

ABOVE, RIGHT With musical collaborators Jack Antonoff (L) and Aaron Dessner (R).

> "We were standing on the edge of the folklorian woods and had a choice: to turn and go back or to travel further into the forest of this music. We chose to wander deeper in"
> TAYLOR SWIFT

where she feels suspicious that everyone who sees him wants him.

For all those who felt aggrieved by the way a relationship ended, 'Closure' was a refusal to be soothed after being so casually dismissed; she simmers that yes, she read his letter, but she doesn't need to be handled, and she's happy nursing her anger.

On *Folklore*, the 13th track was about her grandfather, and on *Evermore*, it was a tribute to her opera-singer grandmother Marjorie Finlay, where she conveys her regret at not asking her all about her life when she was alive, but whose presence she feels around her now.

At the same time as *Evermore* was storming the charts and earning plaudits, she embarked on the process of rerecording her old albums. By placing "Taylor's Version" in brackets after the title, and by including tracks from the Vault, it would ensure that listeners would be attracted to these new releases – it was something that no artist had ever attempted on such a scale. Further, in February 2021, she became the first woman to win Album of the Year three times, when *Folklore* scooped the title. The following year, *Evermore* would also be nominated. This folk era was only the next step in her journey to becoming one of the most successful musicians of all time.

OPPOSITE Taylor Swift makes history again, winning the Album of the Year for the third time at the 2021 Grammys, the first woman to do so.

8

MIDNIGHTS AND THE REREcords

VMA
MTV

"... a nostalgic return to Swift's coming of age, just before she became one of the biggest singers in the world."

THE TIMES

On 11 February 2021 Taylor appeared on *Good Morning America* to announce the upcoming release of *Fearless (Taylor's Version)*. She also revealed it would include never-released Vault tracks to give fans the "full picture" of the album. The rerecordings were not supposed to be new interpretations, but "the same but better", to devalue the original albums that she had no control over.

Rather than starting in chronological order, she began with her second album; it was stronger than her debut, launched her as a global star with the Grammy for Album of the Year, and it included some of her most iconic hits and melodies. Now in her 30s, she was singing the lyrics she wrote as a teenager, but by revisiting them as an adult, she was giving them a universal quality, as if they could speak to all ages.

She went in "line by line" to "listen to every single vocal and think, you know, what are my inflections here. If I can improve upon it, I did. But I really did want this to be very true to what I initially thought of and what I had initially written. But better. Obviously".

Her voice had matured over the years. As well as having dropped the Nashville twang somewhere between *Speak Now* and *1989*, she had evened out the weaknesses in her pitch control. But the differences between the versions were barely noticeable – the odd tweak to sharpen or to provide greater clarity.

As *Pitchfork* described it: "These versions are slightly more polished, like photos touched up on Instagram with a press of a button: The sound is brighter, the mix is clearer, each peal of guitar is sharper."

As well as including 'Today Was a Fairytale', a single she had released to coincide with her role in the movie *Valentine's Day*, there were six new songs on the album, which were recorded with Jack Antonoff and Aaron Dessner.

PREVIOUS SPREAD At the 65th Grammy Awards on 5 February 2023 in Los Angeles. **OPPOSITE** Taylor Swift at the 2023 MTV Video Music Awards.

In tribute to her Nashville roots, she duetted with Maren Morris on 'You All Over Me' and recruited Keith Urban to feature on two "from the Vault" ballads, 'That's When' and 'We Were Happy'.

In 'Mr. Perfectly Fine', seemingly an extension of 'Forever and Always' in its chastising of a man who changes his mind, she reveals a phrase that would become indelible in Taylor lore, and an important touchpoint for 'All Too Well' – "casual cruelty". Listening to these previously unreleased Vault tracks, they offer insight into how she carried phrases and melodies with her, often using them in other places if a track had been dropped from an album in favour of another.

On its release, *Fearless (Taylor's Version)* became the only rerecorded album to ever top the charts, and it also made her the first female artist to have three No. 1 albums in less than a year – after *Folklore* in July 2020 and *Evermore* in December 2020. It also had the biggest first-day album debut of 2021 on Spotify, with over 50 million streams.

Will Hodgkinson, in his review for *The Times*, described it as "wholesome as apple pie" and "a nostalgic return to Swift's coming of age, just before she became one of the biggest singers in the world".

ABOVE Backstage at the 2021 Rock & Roll Hall of Fame induction ceremony for Carole King (second right). Also with Keith Urban, who Taylor recruited for two "from the Vault" tracks, and Nicole Kidman.

Two months after *Fearless (Taylor's Version)* debuted at No. 1 on the *Billboard* 200 chart, she announced its follow-up – *Red (Taylor's Version)*. "This will be the first time you hear all 30 songs that were meant to go on *Red*," she told her followers on social media. "And hey, one of them is even ten minutes long."

The revelation that there was a ten-minute version of 'All Too Well' only added to the anticipation and excitement at the album's imminent release. She described how the album "resembled a heartbroken person. It was all over the place, a fractured mosaic of feelings that somehow all fit together in the end. Happy, free, confused, lonely, devastated, euphoric, wild, and tortured by memories past".

Like *Fearless (Taylor's Version)*, this second rerelease was faithful to the original, bringing back the collaborations with Gary Lightbody and Ed Sheeran and replicating every distinction, including the giggle and the exclamation at the wrap of 'Stay Stay Stay'. The extended version of 'All Too Well' is a further punch at a relationship that had such a visceral effect on Taylor as she was writing *Red*. It flowed with pain and confusion, making digs at his tendency for younger girlfriends, the way he regaled her father with stories as if he were on a late-night talk show, and the heartbreak she felt when he failed to show for her 21st birthday party. It also added further insight into other tracks on the album.

ABOVE At the *All Too Well: The Short Film* premiere at AMC Lincoln Square, 12 November 2021, in New York City.

In 'The Moment I Knew', a bonus track from the original album, she sings of her heartbreak at her lover failing to turn up for an event, and over the ten minutes of 'All Too Well', it is now clear that this event was her 21st birthday. Pained at seeing his daughter pining, her father tells her she should be having fun, but instead all she can think about is this rejection. Their relationship may have disintegrated with the fall of autumn leaves, but it inspired an album that sold seven million copies, and 3.5 million more on its second iteration.

The ten-minute song was accompanied by a short film, written and directed by Taylor, which cast Sadie Sink as the besotted young woman who goes through her "first catastrophic, cataclysmic heartbreak" and Dylan O'Brien as the older man who breaks her heart. Having always had a clear idea of the look and feel of her music videos, Taylor now transitioned into complete ownership as director, further fulfilling her desire to paint the full picture when telling stories.

'All Too Well (Taylor's Version)' would be key to the mammoth success of her rerecordings, while confirming its place as an essential part of her universe when it topped the *Billboard* Hot 100 on its release.

There were nine further "from the Vault" tracks – some that had never previously been released, others

BELOW Taylor with singers Sabrina Carpenter and GAYLE at the American Music Awards, 2022.

OPPOSITE Taylor at the MTV Europe Music Awards, Germany, 2022.

that had been given to other artists. Little Big Town had released 'Better Man' in 2016, while 'Babe' was recorded by Sugarland in 2018.

'Ronan' was initially a charity single for a 2012 Stand Up to Cancer telethon in honour of a little boy, Ronan Thompson, who died of neuroblastoma in 2011. Written from the heartaching point of view of his mother, Maya, Taylor credited her as a cowriter, having been inspired by her blog posts.

'Message in a Bottle' had originally been the first song Taylor wrote with Max Martin and Shellback when working on *Red*, but it ended up on the cutting room floor. Another previously unreleased track, 'Nothing New', became an anxious ballad with Phoebe Bridgers, as they worry over how the industry worships and then discards female musicians.

She teamed up again with Ed Sheeran on 'Everything Has Changed' and a new track, 'Run', and duetted with Chris Stapleton on 'I Bet You Think About Me'. Here she aimed her snark at an ex who is desperate to remain hipster-cool and relevant. In a tie-in with the 'All Too Well' short film, she remembers how she'd felt so young and naive next to his older pretentious friends, but now she imagines him still thinking about her. She is also self-aware in her acknowledgement that he would think her crazy for writing a song about him. It was released as a single to country radio stations, with an accompanying video directed by Blake Lively, in which she played up to her 'Blank Space' persona as she hijacks the wedding of this ex.

Much of the promotion and merchandising focused on the autumnal aesthetics of the album. New artwork showed Taylor posing in a red vintage convertible, wearing a burgundy fisherman's cap and a warm coat, and with her signature red lips. There was a red scarf available for sale on her website, and she partnered with Starbucks to offer a special "Taylor's Latte".

As well as entering the *Billboard* 200 at No. 1 on its release on 12 November, the album won Top Country Album at the *Billboard* Music Awards, and Taylor was named Artist of the Year at the 2022 American Music Awards. At the 65th Annual Grammy Awards, *All Too Well: The Short Film* won Best Music Video, and it also earned her Video of the Year at the MTV Video

OPPOSITE Taylor at the American Music Awards, 2022.

"I'm making more albums at a more rapid pace than I ever did before, because I think the more art you create, hopefully the less pressure you put on yourself."
TAYLOR SWIFT

Music Awards. As she collected her award, dressed in a "bejeweled" gown, she announced the imminent arrival of brand-new music. She followed up with a post explaining that this new album, *Midnights*, would be "the stories of 13 sleepless nights scattered throughout my life".

The idea of a sleepless night peppered her back catalogue, with midnight being namechecked in '22', 'Style', and 'New Year's Day'. The middle of the night was also a time for dreams and desires and terrors in tracks like '...Ready For It? and 'Better Man'. There was the intimate happiness of 'All Too Well', where they dance in the kitchen by the refrigerator light, and in the final words of her album *Lover*, she expresses her wish to be defined by love, not by things that keep her awake at night.

For Taylor, midnight was a vulnerable, lonely time where late-night worries often drove her creative voice. Grappling with the devastation of bad love, the pressures she felt to be the good girl, the expectations placed on her by society and her often overwhelming desire for revenge, she was often kept awake as her mind went to dark places. By choosing this theme for a concept album, with all the codes and references to previous music, it slotted into the retrospective nature of her rerecordings. But it was also completely new material. "Everything on *Midnights* is new work. Nothing is left over from a different album. It might have been ideas or concepts or things I've thought of maybe making in the past, but I didn't write anything until I was making this album."

The roll-out of *Midnights* was a case study in perfect marketing, building up anticipation by dropping clues to its themes and content without releasing a beat of music. Through artwork reveals and a teaser of her upcoming videos, she hinted at not just a fairy-tale "magic at midnight" theme, but a '70s vibe of wood-panelled rooms, garish patterns and plenty of mustard and maroon. Over 17 days, as part of a "Midnights Mayhem" game on TikTok, she spun a vintage bingo cage, pulling out a random number and then revealing its corresponding track name on her retro dial phone.

ABOVE With Phoebe Bridgers at the 2023 iHeartRadio Music Awards. Bridgers features on 'Nothing New' from 2021's Red *(Taylor's Version)*.

Midnights was the first album she recorded entirely with Jack Antonoff, and while its content was dark, it was also supposedly a marker of a happier place, where she said, "I definitely feel more free to create now. And I'm making more albums at a more rapid pace than I ever did before, because I think the more art you create, hopefully the less pressure you put on yourself."

Three hours after the album dropped at midnight on October 21, she put out a deluxe *3am Edition* of the album, which featured seven bonus tracks, creating a further frenzy – helping to break the Spotify record for the most streams of an album in a single day.

The album opens with the woozy 'Lavender Haze', where the first line is an invitation to meet her at midnight, and then launches into further tracks that explore love and desire, regret and angst, and fantasies of revenge. They were all laced with a synth sound and beat that were removed from the folk of her previous releases.

If her other albums had been colour-coded, then *Midnights* ran with it – from 'Lavender Haze' to 'Maroon' to the shimmering gold of 'Bejeweled'. 'Maroon', a darker, more complex shade of red, describes a long-distance romance, from the cheap rosé wine being drunk to the rust symbolic of the distance between phone lines and the purple bruise of a love bite.

She described her inspiration for 'Lavender Haze' as a '50s expression that she had noticed while watching *Mad Men*, and how it meant "that you were in that all-encompassing love glow – and I thought that was really beautiful". She said the haze was also a protection from all the speculation and negativity in the age of social media. "Like my relationship for six years: we've had to dodge weird rumours, tabloid stuff, and we just ignore it."

'Snow on the Beach', a metaphor for strange, awe-inspiring love, was a beautiful, haunting collaboration with Lana Del Rey. Following feedback that Del Rey's

LEFT Taylor Swift accepts the Favorite Pop Album award for Red (Taylor's Version) at the 2022 American Music Awards.

voice wasn't utilized as much as people would have liked, when she released the *Til Dawn Edition* of the album, she included a new version, this time with more of Del Rey's vocals.

There wasn't the big catchy hit of previous albums, although 'Shake it Off' and 'Me!' had felt a little out of step from the overall tone at the time. Instead, the lead single, 'Anti-Hero', a track she described as one of her favourite songs she'd ever written, was a "guided tour" of her mental state as she comes to terms with her own fallibility. She is tormented with worries about her body and ageing, that she might drive away another person in her life, and that she is, in fact, the problem. In one line, taken from an episode of *30 Rock*, she feels like a monster when compared with the other "sexy babies" – the younger stars who threaten to usurp her.

In the music video, set within her '70s world, she is led astray by her bad doppelgänger, has a strange fantasy in which her children are fighting over her will at her funeral and has glitter seeping from wounds. As she explained to director Martin McDonagh in an interview with *Variety*, "There was this weird theme running through the video where I bleed glitter. It's sort of a metaphor for how I don't feel like a normal person. I must have something wrong with me. And it's all the examples of disordered thinking."

Much of the appeal of the album was working out the sheer number of codes in song lyrics and music videos, as the references acted as "invisible strings" between moments in her past. 'Bejeweled', for example, appeared to reference her night at the Met Gala in 2016, when she tired of a thankless relationship and chose to shimmer and shine. The music video, which was a twist on Cinderella, featured the band Haim as the ugly sisters, Laura Dern as the wicked stepmother, and, in Taylor's words, a "psychotic" amount of Easter eggs.

'High Infidelity', from the *3am Edition*, set social media abuzz with a reference to something significant happening on April 29. Was it at Gigi Hadid's party that she first met Joe Alwyn, or was it to do with Calvin Harris dropping 'This I What You Came For' that day – a song, it later transpired, she had written?

OPPOSITE Accepting the award for Best Long Form Video for 'All Too Well' at the 2022 MTV Video Music Awards.

OPPOSITE At the 2023 Grammy Awards where she scooped Best Music Video for *All Too Well: The Short Film*. **LEFT** Landing the double. *Midnights* and 'Anti-Hero' both hit No. 1 in the Official Album and Official Singles charts, respectively.

Throughout the album, she scrutinized her own ambition and what it took for her to achieve success. 'You're On Your Own, Kid' was a reflection of her journey from a small town to the big city, from writing songs in her bedroom to playing them in the parking lot. She also acknowledges the disordered eating that she suffered during her *1989* era, as she struggles in this competitive, bloody world. She juxtaposes the innocence of early fame with a cynicism that life is not the fairy tale she thought it was. There is hope at the end, as she calls for her listeners to make friendship bracelets and to embrace every moment, because a new opportunity can emerge from the worst experiences.

There were also two big revenge tracks, 'Karma' and 'Vigilante Shit', which took aim at those who had wronged her, including the feud with Scooter Braun and Big Machine. In the final, 13th track on the album, 'Mastermind', she faces up to her manipulative, Machiavellian side and attributes it to her own insecurities. She is self-aware enough to admit that the reason for her scheming is because of her loneliness as a child, when her insecurities became an instigator for her future plotting. In the final twist, the boyfriend who she had plotted to be with smiles because he knew about her plans all along.

As part of her promotional tour, she appeared on *The Tonight Show Starring Jimmy Fallon*, where she offered up a hint that she might be touring soon. "I think I should do it," she said, to cheers from the audience. "When it's time," she added cryptically. Just a week later, on 1 November, she made a special announcement that she would be going back on the road with the Eras Tour – an ambitious musical journey that would be the biggest of her career.

9

THE ERAS TOUR

> **"Beatlemania and Thriller have nothing on these shows."**
> PHOEBE BRIDGERS

PREVIOUS SPREAD Taylor performs at SoFi Stadium, Los Angeles on 7 August 2023. **OPPOSITE** Taylor during the *Lover* segment of the Eras Tour.

At the beginning of November 2022, *Midnights* achieved a historic first – every spot in the Top Ten of the *Billboard* Hot 100 was filled by a track from the album. It was just one sign of how Taylor would dominate the music industry in 2023. The pandemic had prevented her from touring three of her albums, *Lover* (2019), *Folklore* (2020) and *Evermore* (2020), and after *Midnights*, the ambitions of the Eras Tour would not only celebrate these albums, but would be a retrospective of her career.

When tickets first went on sale, the unprecedented demand caused Ticketmaster to crash. The record-breaking two million tickets sold on the first day were an early indication of just how overwhelming the global demand would be to see Taylor live.

Taylor trained for six months to prep for the tour, practising her set list by singing while running on the treadmill every day. "I wanted to be so over-rehearsed that I could be silly with the fans, and not lose my train of thought," she said.

This would be the largest undertaking of her career so far, with each three-and-a-half-hour show featuring over 40 songs, 16 costume changes, 6 pyrotechnic displays, a long runway stage and an elevated platform. The atmospheric set design would immerse the audience in her fantasy worlds that represented 17 years' worth of music – the mossy cottagecore of *Folklore* and *Evermore*, the pulsating cityscape of *1989*, the gothic revenge of *Reputation* and the sparkling, shimmering pastels of *Lover*. She zipped from feverishly energetic to introspective acoustic, whether she was strapping a guitar around her neck or seated at the piano.

"They had to work really hard to get the tickets," she said of her fans. "I wanted to play a show that was longer than they ever thought it would be, because that makes me feel good leaving the stadium."

In anticipation of her first show in Arizona, she published photos from rehearsal and announced that she was officially in her "Eras era". The 16 costume changes, custom-made by designers including Versace, Oscar de la Renta and Roberto Cavalli, fed into the looks of her different eras. From the sparkling rainbow leotard by Versace for the opening *Lover* section, to the shimmering Roberto Cavalli black and red snake bodysuit of her *Reputation* era, to the hot pants, bowler hats and slogan tee of *Red*, Taylor's costuming captured the mood and motifs of each of her albums.

Paying tribute to her teen tendency for fairy tales during her 'Love Story' era, Nicole and Felicia designed a sparkling taupe princess gown; the look of '22' was reborn with a new "A lot going on at the moment" T-shirt; there was the hooded cape for the haunting *Evermore* section; and the ethereal white gown of *Folklore*, which gave way to the sparkling, bead-encrusted top and miniskirt for *1989*. At every show, her excited fans styled themselves to match their favourite Taylor era, and with their cowboy boots and fringed dresses, glitter, and heart sunglasses, it was a way of letting their clothes reflect which version they most related to. They also wore and traded friendship bracelets, as Taylor had encouraged in 'You're On Your Own, Kid', to create a new, insider currency of devotion.

When the tour kicked off on 17 March 2023, in Glendale, Arizona, it had a more dramatic impact on the town's businesses than the 2023 Super Bowl, held at the same stadium. The tour gave a massive economic boost to whichever city she was playing in, with hotels and restaurants booked out due to the demands of her vast audience. It was calculated by *The Washington Post* that the average US fan would spend nearly $1,300 at each gig, which included tickets, food and drink, travel and merchandise. Her show in Denver was said to have added $140 million to Colorado's GDP, and her influence on the Philadelphia economy was noted by the Federal Reserve. The "Taylor effect" also led to pleas from the government of Thailand for her to come and perform there. "Beatlemania and *Thriller* have nothing on these shows," said Phoebe Bridgers, as it became the mass cultural moment of a generation.

OPPOSITE Recreating the mossy cottagecore of the Folk era onstage during the Eras Tour.

Another ambitious element of her all-conquering year was bringing the Eras Tour to an even bigger audience by showing it in cinemas for all those who hadn't managed to get tickets. Rather than going with a traditional studio, she made a deal with the world's biggest cinema chain, AMC, to release *Taylor Swift: The Eras Tour*, and when the concert film arrived in cinemas on 13 October, AMC recorded its highest ever single-day ticket sales.

The Eras Tour was one element of what Taylor referred to as "a three-part summer of feminine extravaganza" in 2023, alongside the box-office phenomenon of Greta Gerwig's *Barbie* and Beyoncé's *Renaissance* tour, which took advantage of a similar AMC deal to show it in cinemas.

During Taylor's shows in Nashville in May, her audience screamed in delight at the breaking news that *Speak Now (Taylor's Version)* would be arriving on 7 July, and as she launched into 'Sparks Fly' as the surprise song of the night, the new album cover, with Taylor in a purple dress similar to the one from the original 2010 album, flashed onto the big screen. Shortly after, she posted on her social media accounts that it was arriving "just in time for July 9, iykyk [if you know you know]". It was a little nod to fans about the date mentioned in the lyrics of 'Last Kiss'.

Speak Now (Taylor's Version) debuted at No. 1 on the *Billboard* 200, making her the woman with the most chart-topping albums in history. As with the other rerecordings, she stayed true to the original, except for one controversial line in 'Better than Revenge', where she tweaked the slut-shaming for a less judgemental narrative. The "from the Vault" tracks were once again produced by

BELOW Channelling the 'Lavender Haze' of her *Midnights* era.
OPPOSITE A nod to *Reputation* with the snake bodysuit.

Aaron Dessner and Jack Antonoff, and she collaborated with era-defining emo-rock musicians Fall Out Boy on 'Electric Touch' and Paramore's Hayley Williams on 'Castles Crumbling' to add further 2010 nostalgia.

'When Emma Falls in Love' was a sweet piano ballad that some thought was an ode to her friend, the actress Emma Stone, and 'I Can See You', which boasted an infectious electric guitar, sounded like a mix between the tracks 'Mine' and 'You Belong with Me' as she imagines what she would like to do to the object of her affection. She premiered the music video for 'I Can See You' during her gig in Kansas City, and the spy-themed narrative featured her ex, Taylor Lautner, who had come off well in the song said to have been written about him – 'Back to December'. However, when she performed 'Dear John' as part of her Minneapolis show in June, she urged her fans to show kindness to her famous targets who had not fared quite as well.

On 9 August, in Inglewood, California, the last US date on her tour (before moving on to Mexico and South America), and wearing a long blue dress to match the colour of the summer sky in the album sleeve's new artwork, she announced that *1989 (Taylor's Version)* would be coming soon. It was released on 27 October 2023, nine years after the original turned her into a pop phenomenon. Taylor's version now included five new "from the Vault"

ABOVE Opening night of the Eras Tour on 17 March 2023, during the *Fearless* segment.

tracks, which added extra insight to the romantic longing she felt during this period.

'Is It Over Now?' was about a relationship fracturing due to resentment and betrayal, and a possible hit at Harry Styles with the mention of a blue dress on a boat (matching a paparazzi shot from 2013, picturing her alone on a boat, leaving the Caribbean island that they had been vacationing on), blood on snow alluding to the snowmobile accident from 'Out of the Woods' and his searching for a replacement in every model's bed. 'Say Don't Go' was about the pain of being led on by someone who had no intention of committing, and who left her bleeding from their twisting knife.

'"Slut!"' was a message to her critics that she was too wrapped up in love to care about what they thought. With the flamingo pink sunrise, the aquamarine of the pool and her lovestruck infatuation with the boy who everyone wants, it also had *Lover* vibes.

With its entry at the top of the *Billboard* 200, this release was Taylor's 13th No. 1 album, and she broke her own record for the most streams on a single day on Spotify by an artist. And by achieving her biggest ever sales week for an album, with 3.5 million units sold around the world, it was an even greater success than the original.

"This is the proudest and happiest I've ever felt, and the most creatively fulfilled and free I've ever been," she

ABOVE Taylor Swift: *The Eras Tour* concert movie premieres on 13 October 2023.

Speak
TAYLOR'S
AVAILABL

> "When you say a relationship is public, that means I'm going to see him do what he loves, we're showing up for each other, other people are there and we don't care."
>
> TAYLOR SWIFT

said in late 2023. She had dominated the entire year, saturating every aspect of pop culture as she became a billion-dollar phenomenon.

At the time of the release of *Midnights*, the status of her relationship with Joe Alwyn was still shrouded in mystery. There was gossip and speculation that they were secretly engaged, and even that she was expecting their baby, and the lyrics on the album gave every indication that they were still blissfully together. Although, in 'Lavender Haze' she had expressed frustration at the old-fashioned notions that women were either a one-night stand or a bride, and in 'Midnight Rain' she had reflected on how she had chased fame over marriage.

There was a huge surprise when a source revealed in April 2023 that she and Joe had, in fact, split. It was quickly followed by speculation that she was now dating Matty Healy of The 1975, when he was spotted at some of her shows. This new revelation about Healy left many Swifties angry and upset, given his history of controversial statements, including those aimed at Ice Spice. The rapper later joined Taylor onstage at one of her shows, and they teamed up on a remix of 'Karma', which some believed was Taylor's "damage control" of the situation. Taylor stayed silent about Healy, and with him disappearing from her life over the summer, there would be a new man on the scene – Travis Kelce, the Kansas City Chiefs NFL star. By October they had gone public, and she became

OPPOSITE Announcing the forthcoming release of *Speak Now (Taylor's Version)*, 5 May 2023 in Nashville, Tennessee.

a fixture at his matches. The cameras were focused on her enthusiastically cheering him on in a private box, either next to his mother or with her famous friends. This new romance brought to life the themes of 'Stay Stay Stay' – the love between the good girl and the American football player. Her appearances at his games also brought a massive increase in viewership for the NFL and a cross-pollination of pop and sport.

In an interview in *Time* in December 2023, as she was named the magazine's Person of the Year, she revealed that they had started dating when she found out, via his podcast, that he had turned up to one of her shows wearing a friendship bracelet with his telephone number on the beads.

If her six-year relationship with Joe had been defined by its privacy, she would embrace the full glare of the spotlight with Travis – congratulating him on the pitch, making a surprise appearance on the same episode of *Saturday Night Live*, holding hands when going out to dinner in New York, and during one of her shows in Argentina, she even changed the lyrics to "Karma is the guy on the Chiefs".

As she explained, "When you say a relationship is public, that means I'm going to see him do what he loves, we're showing up for each other, other people are there and we don't care."

The Eras Tour continued into 2024, further building on the mythology of the "Swiftiverse". She won the Grammy for Album of the Year for *Midnights* – making her the first artist ever to win it four times. And that same momentous night, she announced a new album, *The Tortured Poets Department*.

ABOVE Taylor, in a *Reputation*-era Versace corset, and Travis Kelce arriving at the *Saturday Night Live* after-party in October 2023.

LEFT Taylor Swift accepts the Album of the Year award for *Midnights* at the 2024 Grammys.

OPPOSITE Taylor in Versace at the MTV Video Music Awards 2023, where she dominated every category, including Video of the Year for 'Anti-Hero'.

10

THE TORTURED POETS DEPARTMENT

"I think when you go through a heartbreak there's a part of you that thinks, I want a new name, I want a new life, I don't want anyone to know where I've been or know me at all, and that was kind of what that was."

TAYLOR SWIFT

PREVIOUS SPREAD Taylor Swift arrives at the Grammy Awards in Los Angeles, 2024. **OPPOSITE** Taylor announced the upcoming *The Tortured Poets Department* album at the Grammy Awards in February 2024.

From the moment Taylor announced her 11th studio album following her historic win at the Grammys, the major question was what, or whom, it would be about. Would it be a revenge piece on Joe Alwyn? There were hints that she was setting her ire on her ex-boyfriend when she declared, "All's fair in love and poetry."

The new album promised to depict the about-turn of her life after *Midnights*, when she'd gone from a supposedly quiet but contented domesticity away from the public glare to dominating pop culture with her ambitious, highly visible world tour. And she had embarked on a rebound love affair with Matty Healy from The 1975 after ending her six-year relationship with Joe.

Just weeks after the surprise news in April that she and Joe Alwyn had broken up, she was captured at a New York restaurant holding hands with Healy. To go from the clean-cut, private Joe to a raucous provocateur was a shock, particularly when sources claimed that they were in love. After she and Healy split in the summer of 2023, she embarked on the great American romance with Travis Kelce. But, as would be clear in the lyrics of the upcoming album, she bore the scars of a tumultuous two years where her life had shifted in surprising ways.

The inspiration for the album title, at first appearing to be a nod to the movie *Dead Poet's Society*, became even more tantalizing when taking into consideration Joe Alwyn's mention of a group chat with actors Paul Mescal and Andrew Scott called "The Tortured Man Club". Further, in December 2022, Healy had posted a photo with Phoebe Bridgers and Bo Burnham that he had captioned "Gay Poets Society".

Shortly after her Grammys announcement, Taylor unveiled the album's artwork – black and white bedroom-themed photography by Beth Garrabrant, which hinted that this would be a moody, introspective release.

On the cover, she lies on crumpled white sheets in black silk underwear, as if she is lit by the sun streaming through an out-of-shot window. Here she is vulnerable and confessional, and with the aura of Emily Dickinson and Sylvia Plath, her songwriting skills were clearly placed upfront. Poetry had been referenced in past songs, with William Wordsworth and the Romantic poets in 'The Lakes', and in the build-up to the album launch, a genealogy website, likely in collaboration with her team, revealed that Taylor was a very distant relative of Emily Dickinson.

While Taylor had demonstrated the depths of her songwriting with her folk albums and rereleases, there were still people who doubted her talents. There was a perception that because she was a female pop star, her work did not have value. In an interview with the *Los Angeles Times* in January 2022, Damon Albarn, lead singer of Blur, wrongly dismissed her achievements. "She doesn't write her own songs ... I know what cowriting is. Cowriting is very different to writing. I'm not hating on anybody, I'm just saying there's a big difference between a songwriter and a songwriter who cowrites."

His casual assumptions about a female pop star provoked a strong response from Taylor, who called out his "completely false and SO damaging" take. "You don't have to like my songs but it's really fucked up to try and discredit my writing. WOW." In some ways *Tortured Poets* and the focus on songwriting was her answer to these sexist assumptions.

The tracklist also offered a tantalizing glimpse into the themes, and targets, of the album. 'So Long, London' could only be about the London Boy of her *Lover* album, the one who she had set up home with, and whose spirit haunted Cornelia Street. There was 'The Smallest Man Who Ever Lived', sounding like a burn against the man who had never spoken publicly about her, and 'Guilty as Sin?' as a confessional on what went wrong in the relationship.

In further anticipation of the release of the album, Taylor curated her own playlists on Apple under the "five stages of heartbreak". This recategorization of her own music was surprising, particularly when placing under the "denial" playlist the songs that were thought to be about love. It twisted the notions of her relationship with Joe, where tracks like 'Lover' and 'Lavender Haze', supposedly reflective of contentment, were now tainted with doubt.

ABOVE Taylor stepping out with Matty Healy in May 2023 as they leave the Electric Lady recording studio in New York City.

Where love had once burned red, her long-term relationship had been considered a safe, mellow, golden space. But looking back on the lyrics to 'Lavender Haze', as she gazes up at the ceiling in his silence, she hints that he is frustratingly uncommunicative, and that he has no plans to turn those paper rings into a wedding vow.

Finally on 19 April, at midnight, *The Tortured Poets Department* hit streaming sites. Working with her long-time collaborators Jack Antonoff and Aaron Dessner, it shared the synths of *Midnights* and the plucked strings of *Folklore*, while cementing her as a songwriter of fraught emotion who does not shy away from revealing her lowest points.

Just two hours after the album's release, she added to the initial 16 new tracks by releasing another 15, with the whole works now under the title of *The Anthology*. With over two hours' worth of lyrics to be decoded, there were the namechecks – Dylan Thomas, Patti Smith, Stevie Nicks, Clara Bow – as well as some more contemporary pop culture references to Charlie Puth, Pennsylvania pop-punk band The Starting Line and The Blue Nile.

"I'd written so much tortured poetry in the past 2 years and wanted to share it all with you," she wrote on social media. She described it as "an anthology of new works reflecting events, opinions and sentiments from a fleeting and fatalistic moment in time – one that was both sensational and sorrowful in equal measure".

As with *Midnights*, there was no bright, pop lead single – no 'Me!' or 'Shake It Off' – which further shifted her from pop to a more alternative sound. There was a darkness to the lyrics, a grim evocation of prisons, death, psychiatric hospitals and depression, as she painted a picture of an artist struggling to find happiness in herself and to understand her stardom and extreme fame. Each song also had a universal awareness of the transience of relationships, of the numb pain of heartbreak, anxieties and insecurities, and a need for petty revenge, which continued to make her incredibly relatable. If 'Anti-Hero'

LEFT In a corseted denim minidress at the Ned NoMad MTV VMAs after-party in September 2023.

M&T Bank
VISA
AFC CHAMPIONS
CHIEFS ARE
ALL IN

had revealed her struggles with depression, then these 31 tracks would give greater insight into what keeps her awake at night. Songs appear like short stories, building on both fictional and real worlds mined from her own experiences and rendered with poignant, humorous and raw lyrics.

This merging of fact and fiction was evident from the mellow first single, the electro-pop 'Fortnight', featuring Post Malone, which became Spotify's most-streamed song in a single day. The lyrics describe an intense, two-week love affair that she says is ruining her life. She creates an image of herself as drinking too much while being stuck in an endless February (the month when she and Joe split?) while trying to move on. The black and white music video, directed by Taylor, featured Ethan Hawke and Josh Charles, two of the actors from *Dead Poet's Society*, both playing doctors who are giving the depressed Taylor pills and electric shock therapy.

While everyone was expecting the album to be reflective of her six-year relationship, more tracks appeared to be devoted to Matty Healy – a startling response to a short "situationship" that had made such an emotional imprint.

OPPOSITE, ABOVE Celebrating the Kansas City Chiefs winning the Super Bowl in Las Vegas in February 2024.

OPPOSITE, BELOW Taylor kisses Travis Kelce after his Kansas City Chiefs beat the Baltimore Ravens at an AFC Championship NFL game in January 2024.

ABOVE Marketing for *The Tortured Poets Department*.

LEFT Post Malone and Taylor Swift accept the Best Collaboration award for the song 'Fortnight' on stage during the MTV Video Music Awards, New York, 2024. **OPPOSITE** The Eras Tour, 2024.

This time she also took shots at her own fans, with songs 'Who's Afraid Of Little Old Me?' and 'But Daddy I Love Him' aimed at those who chose to criticize her personal life and penned open letters urging her to break up with Healy. Her decisions were hers alone, she was saying, and she did not need moralistic outrage dressed up as advice to tell her what she should do. This was the confusing, at times chaotic life of a woman in her mid-30s who laments that her friends smell of weed and babies; they're either still in their post-adolescent phase or have settled down to have families.

As well as satirizing all the gossip that surrounds her – in the way 'Blank Space' played up to her image as a psycho maneater – 'Who's Afraid Of Little Old Me?' was a bitter attack on those who caged her, tormented her and then turned her into a snarling banshee. It was reminiscent of 'Look What You Made Me Do', where she chooses to kill off the good girl reputation and decides to play up to the persona that's been created. In 'The Albatross', one of the bonus tracks from *The Anthology*, she answers the critics who call her a serial dater, as she sings of men being warned that she is the dangerous albatross who will bring out the jackals, the fake news and the backlash.

'But Daddy I Love Him' owes its title to a line from *The Little Mermaid* (released in 1989, the year of her birth) in which Ariel appeals to her disapproving father, King Triton, that she is in love with a human prince. In this track, she bites back at the pearl-clutchers who chastised her for who she's dating, and she declares that it is this very chaos, his wild personality, that is so intoxicating. Having been in the spotlight since she was a precocious teen, she acknowledges her stunted growth led her to relish the forbidden. She would rather destroy her whole life than listen to all these people who think they know better – the holier-than-thou fans and their wine-guzzling mothers. She even takes delight in feeding the gossip with a tease that she is having his baby. It is just one of several wryly humorous lines across the album.

There are numerous references to cages and prisons. In 'Guilty as Sin?' she equates a long-term relationship to being under house arrest, and now, in her boredom, she emotionally cheats as she fantasizes about another man who sends her The Blue Nile's 'Downtown Lights', a track that was released in 1989. As she describes how she's imagined sleeping with him, it is reminiscent of the *Speak Now* Vault track 'I Can See You'. In 'Fresh Out The Slammer', she has just been released from the prison of a relationship, and after a rough winter of silent dinners, she looks forward to rekindling a lost flame who left the porch light on for her.

During her *1989* days, she and Healy had a flirtation after meeting backstage at one of his concerts in Los Angeles in November 2014, which led to rumours they were dating. Healy publicly denied it at the time. "It is bloody fake. It's all fake. It's all a farce," he told an Australian radio station, Shazam Top 20. He said they had exchanged numbers, but she was the biggest pop star in the world, and he was touring Australia. "So that didn't really happen," he said. "As much as it'd be amazing for me if it did, unfortunately it didn't."

After rumours that Healy had worked with Taylor on some unreleased music for *Midnights*, Taylor made an appearance at The 1975's concert at London's O2 Arena in January 2023, while she was likely still in a long-term relationship with Joe Alwyn. Was this the basis of 'Guilty As Sin?'

'The Smallest Man Who Ever Lived', opening with a

deep, heartbroken sigh, is laced with disappointment and sadness at being ghosted, and Healy-shaped clues are scattered throughout. There's the mention of his Jehovah's Witness suit, like the black suits Healy wears when performing onstage, and that once he had won her over, he became complacent in his stoned oblivion. Similarly, 'My Boy Only Breaks His Favorite Toys' is about a man who smashes up a relationship after he gets what he wants, leaving her broken. In 'Down Bad', he lifts her up in sparkling dust, only to drop her again after experimenting, or toying, with her.

The title track, 'The Tortured Poets Department', paints a picture of a pretentiously tortured artist with tattoos who carries around a typewriter (in an interview with *GQ*, Healy chose the typewriter as one of his essential items), gets stoned and eats seven bars of chocolate. She namechecks Dylan Thomas and Patti Smith in her dismissal that they are not on the level of those tortured talents, and her New York apartment is not the Chelsea Hotel, the legendary bohemian and punk rock magnet where Thomas and Smith both lived at different times.

Maybe the final word on their relationship was in 'Peter', a piano ballad that references the love between Peter Pan and Wendy. The central figure is a boy who can never grow up, despite his promise to come and find her once they are older. The Peter and Wendy symbolism was deployed in 'Cardigan', and while performing this track during the Eras Tour, she had mouthed onstage, "This one is about you. You know who you are. I love you" – the exact same words that Healy had uttered onstage just a few days before.

'Florida!!!' was the most theatrical sound on the album, and it was a powerhouse track of female musicians, with Florence Welch of Florence and the Machine playing instruments as well as singing chorus. The Orange State was also namechecked in 'Fortnight' as a place of refuge, and it was also where she performed for the first time after her breakup announcement, changing the set list from 'Invisible String' to 'The 1'.

Swift explained to iHeartRadio that the song was inspired by a *Dateline* episode about criminals who escape to Florida after they've committed a crime, again following the prison metaphor of a stifling long-term

OPPOSITE Florence Welch of Florence and the Machine, 2023.

relationship and the release that follows its end.

"I think when you go through a heartbreak there's a part of you that thinks, I want a new name, I want a new life, I don't want anyone to know where I've been or know me at all, and that was kind of what that was," she said.

Habitually, Taylor saves track five for the emotional punches of her albums ('Dear John', 'All Too Well', 'The Archer', 'My Tears Ricochet'), and on *Tortured Poets* it was 'So Long, London'. Opening with the sound of church bells, it was a sad follow-up to 'London Boy', where she had relished her time hanging out in the pub and going to Camden Market. Now she's a lonely figure in their home in Hampstead Heath, and accompanied by synths and piano, she paints a gloomy picture of a dying relationship, where she admits defeat despite trying hard to revive it with CPR. Similar in its theme to 'You're Losing Me', a bonus track from *Midnights* where she laments how unmarriageable she is, in 'So Long London' she feels like she is dying on the altar while she waits for something to happen. She is angry that he took her youth (her 20s and early 30s), and that the stitches have now come undone, which is reminiscent of 'Glitch', where she clung to him like a stitch.

London also makes an appearance in 'The Black Dog', where she tracks an ex's phone to find he's gone to the Black Dog pub in Vauxhall with a young woman. Immediately after the album's release, Swifties made their own pilgrimages to this real-life bar.

When Taylor embarked on the Eras Tour, it was assumed she was at her happiest. She appeared onstage flashing a dazzling smile and shimmering in her stage costumes. During her Foxborough, Massachusetts show in May 2023, in which she performed despite the heavy rain, she even told the crowd before performing the surprise song 'Question ...?': "I've just never been this happy in my life, in all aspects of my life, ever before ... It's not just the tour. I just sort of feel like my life finally feels like it makes sense."

But this is at odds with the mood of 'I Can Do It with a Broken Heart', where despite the glitter under the lights, she is heartbroken and depressed, but she is determined to put on the best show for her fans. By the end of the track, to a soaring, optimistic beat, Taylor

OPPOSITE The lyrics of 'I Can Do It with a Broken Heart' are a nod to Taylor's sparkling performance on the Eras Tour.

exclaims gleefully that she's miserable and nobody knows. Again, her fans might think they know her, but they don't fully understand what's happening in her life. The song recalls a moment from Katy Perry's 2012 documentary *Part of Me: The Movie*, when the pop star receives a text message from her husband asking for a divorce, just as she prepares to perform a huge concert. She wipes away the tears, plasters on a smile, and rises onto the stage.

Fame and the fickle nature of celebrity, particularly for female artists, is a common theme of Taylor's. In 'Nothing New', a Vault track from *Red (Taylor's Version)* featuring Phoebe Bridgers, she confessed to her fears at being replaced. In 'Clara Bow', she further reflects on this pressure, that there's always a new "It" girl waiting in the wings. At times, Taylor has been compared with Stevie Nicks, possessing the same hair and lips as the singer in the mid-'70s, and by the end of the track, a new girl is being told she looks just like Taylor Swift, yet she has the edge that the existing Taylor lacks. It was the first time (with the exception of the self-deprecation in '22' and being told she looked like an American singer in 'Invisible String') that she acknowledged her own name within her lyrics.

There was a confusion of emotions throughout the album, and amidst the retrospection were happy songs that appeared to reference her relationship with Travis Kelce. 'The Alchemy' is heavy on its American football references, as she sings of winning streaks, touchdowns and seizing the crown. In 'So High School', she rejoices in the simplicity of dating – of intimate moments while he and his friends play *Grand Theft Auto*, of watching *American Pie* and of feeling like a giddy teenager.

The Tortured Poets Department also revels in glorious pettiness, as she brings up old feuds. In 'thanK you aIMee', a country-tinged revenge song set in a small town, she goes back to the capital-lettered clues of her early album liner notes to take aim at Kim Kardashian. This spray-tanned, worshipped figure has caused her so much misery that even her mother wishes her dead – yet Taylor acknowledges that this pain has helped drive her success. 'Cassandra', with a piano riff and similar vibe to that of 'Mad Woman', refers to the Greek myth of Cassandra, who was disbelieved despite her prophecies. Here she says she tried to warn people about her enemy who filled her cell with snakes, but instead, the trolls turn on her.

The final track of *The Tortured Poets Department: The Anthology* is 'The Manuscript', and with its simple piano,

"An ultra-confident, ballad-heavy, poetic yet grounded reflection on love in all its forms."

THE TIMES

ABOVE The artwork for *The Tortured Poets Department.*
OPPOSITE Book spines featuring song titles on display at Spotify's Taylor Swift pop-up at The Grove in Los Angeles, 2024.

it comes back full circle to the extended version of 'All Too Well'. The short film was framed like a novel about a doomed relationship between a 30-year-old man and a younger woman. In the final shots, the female protagonist, now older, reads from its pages at her book launch. Here, in the lyrics to 'The Manuscript'', she reflects on that time in her life, when she wished she could be 30 too, sophisticated enough to make coffee in a French press, but instead is dismissed by him for her youth. After their breakup, she is so devastated that all she is able to do is eat breakfast cereal and sleep in her mother's bed, but she is told that writing about it will be healing. Now all that remains is the manuscript, and when she sends it out into the world, it is no longer hers. On release of *The Anthology*, she released a statement that this chapter of her life was now "closed and boarded up". Once the saddest story is spoken, "we can be free of it. And then all that's left behind is the tortured poetry".

Hours after the album dropped, it received a round of five-star reviews, including from *Rolling Stone*. She shared it on Instagram with the caption, "And that's the closest I've come to my heart exploding" – a line from the titular track.

It wasn't all glowing reviews; there were criticisms that the themes had all been heard before. *Paste* chose to keep their scathing reviewer anonymous because, due to the ferocity of Taylor's fans, "in 2019 when *Paste* reviewed *Lover*, the writer was sent threats of violence from readers who disagree with the work".

Still, the album was a record-breaker, and despite not giving any interviews to promote it, she made Spotify history as the most-streamed artist in a single day, with over 200 million plays. According to *Billboard*, it also broke the record as the most-streamed album ever, proving that Taylor Swift was an unstoppable cultural force.

11

THE ERAS TOUR REVAMPED

TAYLOR'S VERSION
HAZE
ERAS

"I never thought that writing one line about friendship bracelets would have you guys all making friendship bracelets, making friends and bringing joy to each other. That is the lasting legacy of the tour."
TAYLOR SWIFT

PREVIOUS SPREAD The Eras Tour, 2024.
OPPOSITE A fan shows off her friendship bracelets at the Eras Tour, 2024.

After the release of *Tortured Poets*, Taylor began a new leg of the Eras Tour in Europe. It kicked off with four nights in Paris, where she revealed a revamped set list and a whole new segment devoted to her new music. With another album to squeeze in, she was forced to make cuts in order to whittle down her career to 46 songs. She condensed *Folklore* and *Evermore* into a single "Folkmore" chapter, and she shifted the *Red* section forward. She dropped a number of beloved favourites to include new songs 'Fortnight', 'Down Bad', 'But Daddy I Love Him', 'Who's Afraid Of Little Old Me?', 'The Smallest Man Who Ever Lived' and 'I Can Do It with a Broken Heart'. She also introduced new outfits, including a sparkling red Versace bodysuit for the opening, a black dress with silver tassels for the *Fearless* tracks and a new T-shirt for performing '22', this time emblazoned with the words: "This is not Taylor's Version." For the *Tortured Poets Department* section, she wore a cream ball gown, billowing around her like white paper scrawled with black lettering, and to her Paris audience she described this segment as "female rage, the musical", an expression that her team swiftly applied for trademark.

She also told her Paris crowd that she was so lucky to launch the European leg in "the most beautiful, romantic city in the world". There were further shows across Europe, including in Edinburgh, Liverpool, Cardiff and London, and then on to Amsterdam and dates in Germany, Switzerland and Italy. At London's Wembley Stadium, Tom Cruise and Prince William and his children were just some of the famous guests who watched her perform alongside an audience of 90,000 fans for each of the three nights in July. She also surprised everyone when Travis Kelce, dressed in top hat and tuxedo, took to the stage for 'I Can Do It With A Broken Heart'. London was awash with Swifties dazzling in their sparkling outfits as they snapped up merchandise from the official shop, exchanged friendship bracelets and made a pilgrimage to take selfies at the Black Dog pub. But the show had to come to an end at some point, and she announced it would finish in North America in December 2024.

The hugely ambitious Eras Tour cemented Taylor as the most important female performer of the twenty-first century, the most lauded songwriter and the most talked about woman in the world. With the accolades, there would inevitably be backlash as well. She was criticized for her political stance as she became the target of a bizarre conspiracy theory in which her and Travis's romance was supposedly being used by the Democrats to bolster President Biden's re-election; her private jet usage drew the ire of environmentalists, including Just Stop Oil campaigners; and she regularly provoked eyerolls from those who thought her too bland or too obsessed about her relationships. But Taylor's gift is her connection to her audience and the relatability of her lyrics to people of all ages. It is the magic of her songcraft, the catchiness of her hooks and the soaring emotion of her ballads, all of which leave millions of fans coming back for more.

Across her genre-shifting career, she has revealed her story through music, using her experiences to shape her own narrative worlds. Her song lyrics can be pieced together like an Agatha Christie novel, leading to a fixation by her fan base on every minuscule detail or clue she drops. As a businesswoman, she built an empire worth over $1 billion, and she continues to dominate news headlines and social media as she deftly utilizes every modern marketing tool at her disposal. Now that she has reclaimed her own music and boosted global economies, we can only imagine how she will continue to be a guiding light for female musicians, and how both her truth and her fiction will demonstrate the power of storytelling.

OPPOSITE A young fan at The Eras Tour, 2024.

METHOD DRESSING AND WARDROBE

At the Golden Globes in January 2024, Taylor arrived on the red carpet in a metallic green Gucci gown covered in sequins that resembled snake scales. As she made the whole place shimmer, speculation went into overdrive that she was now channelling her *Reputation* era.

At this point, there were now only two more rereleases to go – her debut and *Reputation* – and as she was photographed around New York, visiting restaurants with friends and leaving Electric Lady Studios, she appeared to drop hints through her wardrobe choices as to which was up next. There was the green velvet dress by Scottish brand Little Lies, worn with snake-motif Jean Paul Gaultier and Jimmy Choo boots to meet Blake Lively and friends at Brooklyn's Lucali pizza restaurant; she wore a black Versace corset with the signature gold Medusa emblem on its straps when attending the *SNL* after-party in October 2023 with Travis Kelce; and on a night out with her female friends, including Selena Gomez and Sophie Turner, in October 2023, she flashed a Mazin snake ring. It all screamed *Reputation*.

Then she surprised everyone at the Grammys in February when her white strapless Schiaparelli couture gown and black opera gloves became the purposeful, monochrome choice to announce *The Tortured Poets Department*. The folds of white fabric, as clean as the blank pages of a notebook, also matched the moody black and white photos of the cover art, with Taylor lying on crumpled white sheets, alone and introspective, melancholic in her solitude.

As she reevaluated her works during her rerecordings, she adopted a form of "method dressing" to offer an extra level of subliminal messaging.

Taylor has long employed costume as a silent language to convey a particular mood or time in her life. As emphasized and celebrated through the Eras Tour, Taylor's career is divided into distinctive chapters with their own colour and style, and she typically matches her wardrobe to the content and feel of her albums. By taking on the aesthetics that reflected each of her eras, she knew that Swifties would have fun with the codebreaking to guess which rerecording she was working on.

"I can look back at an old photo and tell you roughly what year it's from," Taylor told *Vogue* in 2016. "Going through different phases is one of my favorite things about fashion. I love how it can mark the passage of time. It's similar to my songs in that way – it all helps identify where I was at in different points of my life."

With every step in her career, Taylor tweaked her style – smoothing out the curls, swapping the sundresses and cowboy boots for fringed dresses and romantic chiffon, and then going funkier with Wayfarer sunglasses and hot pants for *1989*. From the black and red of *Reputation*, she emerged as a pastel butterfly for *Lover*, but during the pandemic, working on her folk albums, she had limited opportunities to use fashion, and instead chose plaid shirts and vintage frontier dresses, like the ones she enjoyed dressing up in with friends, to reflect the lockdown mood.

Costume is a vital component for the construction of a pop star, and Taylor shifted and adapted with every reinvention of her sound. Her initial image was one tied to country music, and as the pretty teen icon from Nashville, she was fresh and approachable in her sundresses and boots, helping her to connect with teenage girls who could easily

PREVIOUS SPREAD Taylor sparkles in red Vivienne Westwood at the 2025 Grammy Awards.

OPPOSITE Metallic green Gucci at the Golden Globes, January 2024.

copy her style. In the music video for 'Our Song', she is as girlish as Jessica Simpson, with her blonde hair in curls, lip gloss and glittery nail polish, which she applies to her toes in her bedroom. For her first red carpet appearance, 2006's Academy of Country Music Awards, she chose a floral handkerchief BCBG dress, a favourite label in those early years, which she teamed with cowboy boots. It was an important event, designed to set her up as the teen country star to watch, and while she continued with the bohemian sundresses for magazines, she transitioned to tulle and sequin prom-style dresses for award appearances, as if they were the wardrobe dream of a teenage girl, imagined in the pages of her diary.

"I wasn't trying to make people dress a certain way, but seeing girls coming to my shows wearing sundresses and cowboy boots and curling their hair is one of my favourite experiences ever because I remember when I was weird for dressing the way that I dressed and I was weird for having curly hair. It's really fun to see that I'm not that weird anymore," she told *Marie Claire* in 2009.

With *Fearless*, she embraced her love of romantic history, wearing Renaissance-style gowns while performing 'Love Story'. Her strapless gowns, such as the Reem Acra gown worn to the Country Music Association Awards in 2009, glittered with sequins and flowed with tulle, as if she were stepping out of her own fairy tale.

She was still singing country, but onstage she now wore sparkling fringe dresses that matched her guitar, and straight boots rather than the cowboy style. By the time *Speak Now* was released in October 2010, she was a global star with her first Grammy for Album of the Year under her belt. Her aesthetic was still soft and romantic, but instead of the fringed dresses, she was choosing sweetheart necklines and flared skirts, worn with red lips and soft, pinned-back hair for a vintage pin-up style. Purple was also the colour of the album – on the cover she wore a strapless purple chiffon (by Reem Acra), and a short purple chiffon dress with a sweetheart neckline was a popular part of her custom-made *Speak Now* tour costumes by Susan Hilferty. Her love for romantic vintage was also evident in the white lace frontier dress when performing 'Mean' with a banjo – a look that would be revived in the 'Cardigan' and 'Willow' music videos.

The red lips would become her signature look for her third album, *Red*, when she straightened her hair and chose a simplified hipster wardrobe of high-waisted shorts and blouses, bowler hats and brogues. With paparazzi interest in her love life also ramping up, she was snapped with boyfriends in the autumnal wardrobe that would be the staple of this era – the knitted scarves and hats, duffel coats and plaid shirts.

Over the summer of 2012, as she was putting together *Red*, Taylor was dating Conor Kennedy, and so she dressed to impress the Kennedy clan in Cape Cod with her polka-dot swimsuits and striped shirts, yacht-themed sweaters and full skirts. This was another form of method dress that conveyed her appreciation of the history of the family, which would inspire the track 'Starlight'.

In the lead-up to the release of *Red*, she teased the themes of the album with her wardrobe choices: the red lace French Connection dress worn to the iHeartRadio Music Festival in Las Vegas in September 2012; the belted tomato-red dress after her appearance on the *Late Show with David Letterman* on 23 October 2012; and, over the next few days, arriving for interviews in New

OPPOSITE Wearing green velvet to meet friends in Brooklyn in January 2024.

York in a red Fay single-breasted coat and Kate Spade red sweater. She also unveiled a more sophisticated look at the Country Music Association Awards in November 2012, in a Jenny Packham gown with red flowers embroidered onto beige lace.

"I'm not going to sit there and say, 'Oh, I wish I hadn't had corkscrew-curly hair and worn cowboy boots and sundresses to award shows when I was 17; I wish I hadn't gone through that fairy-tale phase where I just wanted to wear princess dresses to awards shows every single time,'" she told *Elle* in 2015. "Because I made those choices. I did that. It was part of me growing up."

By the time she entered her *1989* era, she had constructed a new look for an exciting new time in her life, where she was young, talented and single in New York City. "I had tried on something new that fit really well," she said of the experimentation in *Red*. "So for this album I decided, 'Hey, that thing I tried last time? I'm going to make my whole wardrobe into that.'"

She bobbed and straightened her hair, styled it with a sweeping fringe, and was frequently pictured stepping out in short skirts and heels, shorts and crop tops, and with the latest "It" bag dangling from her arm. There were pieces from Topshop, Dolce & Gabbana and Miu Miu, as if she was having fun in a city where cutting-edge fashion was on her doorstep. With the album released in autumn 2014, she was snapped leaving her New York apartment in a series of preppy styles to suit the changing season: plaid skirts and dresses, knitted berets, lace-up boots, and duffel coats. "There's something about New York that makes me want to dress nicely," she told *Vogue*.

The '80s theme of her album melded with the bright colours, funky Wayfarer sunglasses, crop tops and miniskirts. This new look was first unveiled in the Mario Testino photos for her cover shoot for *British Vogue*, styled in an acid green Christopher Kane sweater, pink and white Miu Miu and Valentino and with her hair chopped and funkily styled.

At awards shows, she was also more cutting edge, choosing designers like Elie Saab for the Grammy Awards in February 2015. She first met Joseph Cassell Falconer, a Nashville stylist, when he assisted her on the *Speak Now* tour, and he helped shape these more daring red carpet and tour looks. Her preppy daywear contrasted with her event looks, where she was sexier and more experimental, such as the edgy aqua Mary Katrantzou jumpsuit worn to the 2014 VMAs. The butt-skimming outfit was an about-turn for Taylor, who, at that point, was known for being demure and conservative.

At the Grammy Awards in 2016, she marked the end of the *1989* era in a hot pink and orange midriff-revealing Versace. The experimentalism culminated at the Met Gala in 2016, with a new look of bleached hair, black lips and a silver snakeskin dress. The unveiling of this new image tied into a fan theory of a lost album that was to be called *Karma*. Taylor had fallen into a pattern of releasing a new album every two years, and so when she unveiled her platinum blonde, rockier and shimmering silver look, first on the cover of *Vogue* in May 2016 and at the Met Gala later that month, it was thought that this was a signal for a new era. This was backed by a comment during her '73 Questions' video with *Vogue* in April 2016

ABOVE, LEFT Taylor in Hyannisport with Conor Kennedy in July 2012.
ABOVE, RIGHT Collecting her award for Female Vocalist of the Year at the 2009 CMA Awards, in glittering Reem Acra.
BELOW Wearing the purple dress during the Speak Now tour.

iHeart
iHeart
iHeart
iHeart
iHeart
iHeart
iHeart
iHeart
iHeart

that her life lesson is that "karma is real". But as she fell under attack due to her numerous feuds, the album was supposedly scrapped. In the music video for 'The Man', she further hinted at its existence when her male persona pees against a wall with the titles of all her albums in graffiti, including *Karma*.

After she fled from the public eye due to the intense pressure, she returned with a vengeance for *Reputation*. The grey Pinko stone-washed cotton sweatshirt for the album cover, and the Marc Jacobs camouflage hooded jacket, was a statement of war. Her music video for 'Look What You Made Me Do' was loaded with snake jewellery, including Bulgari Serpenti bracelets and necklaces, worn with a red, dressing-gown-style dress from Balmain, the Fausto Puglisi white shirt splashed with red as if covered in blood as she wields a chainsaw, and the Balenciaga patent leather hooded cape, black cut-out bodysuit, and chokers and cuffs, like bondage-wear.

Her promotional appearances during this time were similarly loaded with snake jewellery, heavy combat boots, hoodies, leg-revealing black shorts and shimmering hooded dresses and playsuits. The whole look was softened for the 'Delicate' music video as she wears a sapphire Naeem Khan fringed dress and dances as if no one can see her. Slowly, colour began to re-emerge in her wardrobe with cut-off denims and pink hoodies as she prepared for the *Reputation* tour.

In anticipation of a new album, *Lover*, there were some little clues to her new direction, beginning in March 2019. She was spotted in Beverly Hills in a pale blue Zadig & Voltaire sweater decorated with white hearts and thunderbolts, and then a rainbow-sequinned playsuit and butterfly heels at the iHeartRadio Music Awards. With the single-shoulder rainbow-sequinned bodysuit while performing 'Me!' for the 2019 Billboard Awards in Las Vegas, she fully emerged from her cocoon in a cloud of pastel – candyfloss pink, baby blue, lilac – not only symbolizing a personal reawakening but also reflecting her new, outspoken LGBTQ+ support.

In February 2020, to mark the release of 'The Man' music video, where she disguised herself with prosthetics to play a confident, privileged alpha male, she chose power-dressing for public appearances: a tweed bustier, tailored pants and checked coat by Carmen March for the premiere of her *Miss Americana* documentary at the Sundance Film Festival in January 2020, and a pinstripe shirt and blazer combo at the *NME* Awards in February 2020.

Then the pandemic struck, and confined to her house in London, she was only visible on Instagram and through the artwork for *Folklore* and *Evermore*, where she was photographed alone in woodland in Stella McCartney checked coats. As part of the publicity for the first single, 'Cardigan', she produced a cable-knit yachting cardigan for her own clothing range, which famous friends Suki Waterhouse, Kaia Gerber and Halsey all modelled on Instagram at the end of July 2020.

Finally, she was able to make her first public appearance at the Grammy Awards in March 2021, dressed in a floral Oscar de la Renta to suit the boho of *Evermore*.

In the lead-up to *Midnights* in autumn 2022, there was a switch in aesthetic to a '70s palette of orange and white stripes, maroons, blues and muddy greens as she unveiled the tracklist on TikTok. For the promotion of 'Lavender Haze',

OPPOSITE Taylor capturing the aesthetics of *Red* at the 2012 iHeartRadio Music Festival in Las Vegas.
OVERLEAF, LEFT Taking risks in the Mary Katrantzou jumpsuit at the 2014 VMAs.
OVERLEAF, RIGHT With high school friend Abigail Anderson at the 2015 Grammy Awards, in Elie Saab.

VIDEO
MUSIC
AWARDS

CMA
AWARDS

BMI

there was a fluffy lavender faux fur coat by Free People, which was replicated in the Eras Tour with a custom-made Oscar de la Renta version. 'Karma', from *Midnights*, harked back to the mood of *Reputation*, and at the iHeartRadio Music Awards in Los Angeles on 27 March 2023, she wore a dazzling hooded jumpsuit by Alexandre Vauthier to collect her Innovator Award. While some thought it was a clue that *Reputation (Taylor's Version)* was on its way, it was more a signal that the remix with Ice Spice and its accompanying music video would be released next.

After announcing that *1989 (Taylor's Version)* was set to come out in October 2023, her wardrobe took on the sky blues of its artwork. She was spotted in New York in September in an aqua Alaïa skater minidress and Prada platform sandals; the next day, a denim corseted minidress at the MTV Video Music Awards after-party; and for the premiere of *The Eras Tour* concert film on 11 October 2023, a pale blue strapless Oscar de la Renta dress.

Her romance with Travis Kelce brought in a new mode of dress – championing his football games with Kansas City Chiefs sweaters, red jackets draped down one shoulder and red lipstick to match the team colours. She had a history of using red as a symbol of passion and intense love, and now she had another reason to wear it.

Stepping out with him in New York on 15 October, her leather miniskirt, Jean Paul Gaultier sheer black and green floral top and heavy black Louis Vuitton ankle boots were the first supposed clue that *Reputation (Taylor's Version)* was coming. Further, for the *Time* cover, her black leotard and make-up, with the red lips, pared-down eyes and stringy hair, appeared to reference the cover of the 2017 album. However, in February 2024, she entered into her *Tortured Poets* era of stark black and white, including the Toni Matičevski corseted gown for the 'Fortnight' music video, which, like the Schiaparelli gown at the Grammys, resembled crumpled bedsheets.

Her story has now been set by her clothing. Having fully embraced method dressing, the clues for future music will always be found in the mood of what she wears.

ABOVE, LEFT In Jenny Packham at the 2012 Country Music Awards.

ABOVE, RIGHT Unveiling what might have been the Karma look, at the BMI Pop Awards in Beverly Hills in May 2016.

BELOW, LEFT At the NME Awards in February 2020, channelling 'The Man'.

BELOW, RIGHT At the premiere of the *Miss Americana* documentary at the Sundance Film Festival in January 2020.

OVERLEAF, LEFT In a ruffled lavender minidress by Raisa & Vanessa at the 2019 Billboard Music Awards.

OVERLEAF, RIGHT In the Alexandre Vauthier hooded jumpsuit at the iHeartRadio Music Awards in March 2023.

LAS VEGAS

pink

A GUIDE TO THE SWIFTIVERSE

One of the reasons Taylor Swift is so beloved is the "Swiftiverse" she has created through her songwriting, where she threads her lyrics with reoccurring imagery and symbolism, like the self-described mastermind that she is. Songs drip with a painterly use of colour, and there's the symbolic contrast between the big city and the small town, of adulthood and innocence, and of using cars as an escape or as a crash and burn. They are sprinkled with stardust, or they float with the imagery of diving into oceans or lighting a match and going up in flames. They are also peppered with real experiences and real places, like Cornelia Street or the Black Dog pub, as she shares her life with her listeners. Here's a list of the most common subjects that reoccur time and again.

AUTUMN The album *Red* was a whole autumn mood, where in the title track, reckless love is the colour of autumn leaves – at their brightest before they fall. And in 'All Too Well', she is so besotted that they mirror her relationship falling into place. It is the most romantic but bittersweet of times, when in 'Cornelia Street', the autumn air comes through open windows, and in 'Marjorie' the autumn chill wakes her up. It is also tinged with nostalgia. In 'The Best Day', her childhood memories are of visiting the pumpkin patch in her big coat, and she begins to understand that, like the trees before the autumn, we change as we grow up, and her mother is always a comforting presence.

BARS In 'Delicate', he messages her to meet at a dive bar on the East Side; in 'So It Goes', she is now in this bar, desperate to be alone with him; and in 'Cardigan' she remembers kissing in cars and downtown bars. She's drunk in the back of the car after an evening in a bar in 'Cornelia Street', and in 'Cruel Summer', she's crying coming home from the bar. But in 'Invisible String', she's thankful for that dive bar that tied him to her. In 'Hits Different', she slurs his name at the bar and stops receiving invitations.

BONES These are the deepest, rawest, most vulnerable parts of the body. In 'Closure', knowing him cuts her down to the bone, and in 'My Tears Ricochet', he can go for blood but she tells him he would still miss her in his bones. In 'Chloe or Sam or Sophia or Marcus', he saw her bones with someone new. 'Its Time to Go' is about moving on, and as she bravely runs, he stays sitting on his throne in his palace of bones. In 'So Long, London', she is worn down to the bones and has stopped CPR because the spirit of the relationship has gone.

CAGES In 'This Is Me Trying', she blames herself for self-sabotage because the cages were in her head. In 'Guilty as Sin?' the cage had once been fine, but the boredom is bone-deep, and she dreams of breaking the lock to escape onto the ocean rocks. In '"Who's Afraid of Little Old Me? they caged her and called her crazy, but now, like a circus animal, she shows her teeth, just as they taught her. In 'I Know Places', there's a fame analogy of being hunted by those with guns and cages.

CAR CRASHES *1989* drips with car crash imagery, from 'Style' to 'All You Had to Do Was Stay', where he drove them off the road. In 'Getaway Car', she uses the image of criminals making an escape to represent a doomed rebound relationship, which she ultimately runs out on, and similarly in 'The Bolter', it starts with a kiss but ends with a car speeding out the drive. In 'Red', fast, burning love is like a Maserati going down a one-way street, and in 'I'm Gonna Get You Back', she's an Aston Martin that he steered straight into the ditch. In 'The Smallest Man Who Ever Lived', he crashed her party and his rental car.

CARD GAMES In 'Say Don't Go', she asks to see his cards and threatens to fold unless he tells her not to go. In 'Delicate', she references card sharks and playing games

PREVIOUS SPREAD Posing with fans at the 2019 MTV Video Music Awards, 2019.

as she wonders if he is leading her on. The antagonist in 'Dear John' also plays twisted chess games that she can never win. But it can also be positive; in 'Gold Rush', his hair falls into place like dominoes, and in 'Mastermind', those dominoes also fall in a line.

CHRISTMAS Given her birthday is just before Christmas, this time of year is bittersweet and nostalgic, and it forms a background for *Evermore*'s 'Champagne Problems' and ''Tis the Damn Season'. In 'Begin Again', she is endeared by someone on the rebound who speaks of the Christmas movies he watches with his family every year. In 'Lover', the Christmas lights stay up until January, but it can be a lonely time. In 'The Moment I Knew', it's her birthday, and Christmas lights glisten as she watches and waits, hoping he will turn up. And in 'I Look in People's Windows', she observes Christmas parties from the outside as she mourns the loss of a love.

CLOTHES Taylor frequently mentions clothing as a means of painting a character or situation. Even when singing about stuck Chevy trucks in 'Tim MGraw', she eulogizes her little black dress and old faded blue jeans.

She's the dorky girl in T-shirts and sneakers, set apart from the other high-maintenance girl in her short skirts and high heels in 'You Belong with Me'. In 'Speak Now', the bride she's jealous of wears a gown shaped like a pastry, floating down the aisle like a pageant queen. She is also scathing about the girl in 'Better Revenge', whose vintage dresses don't give her dignity.

There's the magic of the ball gowns, the lights and the party in 'Love Story'. 'Starlight' has the feel of 'Enchanted' as she sings of a magical night dancing with finely dressed people. But sometimes this adds to the heartbreak. In 'Dear John', she's the girl in the dress crying the whole way home. And in 'The Moment I Knew', she's in a party dress and red lipstick, waiting hopelessly for the guy to arrive.

She's always liked a guy in simple jeans and T-shirts. In 'You Belong with Me', he wears old jeans; in 'Today Was a Fairytale', he wears a grey T-shirt; in 'All Too Well', it's a plaid shirt; and in 'Delicate', he wears dark jeans and Nikes. This contrasts with the smug ex of 'Mr Perfectly Fine' in the well-pressed suit. In 'Blank Space', she describes the men she lures as "new money, suit and tie", and she can see them coming. In 'The Smallest Man Who Ever Lived', he wears a Jehovah's Witness suit. The suited finance guy, for Taylor, is not as real as the one in jeans and a T-shirt.

Clothes have memories – the scarf with her scent still lingering on it in 'All Too Well', and the old cardigan in 'Cardigan' that still carries memories 20 years later. In 'Begin Again', the one good thing about a breakup is she can wear high heels again, reminiscent of a famous quote by Nicole Kidman.

For *1989*, she is more sophisticated, with the cherry lips, dressed like a fantasy, but she is a nightmare in 'Blank Space'. In 'Style', she has the classic red lips and tight little skirt, while he is James Dean in a white T-shirt, his long hair slicked back. In 'Wildest Dreams', she is in a nice dress, with red lips and rosy cheeks, as the sun sets, and then his clothes are in her room. This is the first sexual hint in her songs. In 'So It Goes...' she wears him like a necklace, and in 'Dress', she only bought the dress so he could take it off. In 'Cardigan', he wears Levi's and has his hand under her sweatshirt as they drunkenly dance under the streetlights. In 'Gold Rush', the Eagles T-shirt is hanging from the door. In 'Cardigan', she remembers the vintage tee, brand-new phone, and high heels on cobblestones, and there is also a sequin smile and black lipstick, which is similar to what she was wearing at the Met Gala.

In 'Happiness', she moves on after a destructive relationship, and thinking of the dress she wore at midnight, she'll leave all those memories behind.

Clothing can be vicious – in 'You're on Your Own, Kid', like Carrie, she's targeted by the bullies at the prom in her blood-soaked gown. In 'Vigilante Shit', she dresses for revenge. In 'Bejeweled', she decides she's leaving him at home to go out in a sparkling gown that will make the whole place shimmer. In 'I Can Do It with a Broken Heart', she's in her glittering prime, the light reflecting her sequins as she puts on her best face.

COLOUR Taylor's lyrics are loaded with colour symbolism, with red as the fire of dangerous love, grey for ambiguity, the blue and golden safety of a more stable love, and then the lavender and maroon of in between.

In 'Cold as You', from her debut, an emotionally unavailable guy paints his walls a shade of grey, and in 'Tim McGraw', there was a first mention of blue eyes (her own), which are said to shine like the Georgia night sky. In *Red*, she fully embraces the symbolism. In the titular track, dangerous, crazy love comes in fiery autumn colours that can only last a short time. To lose love is to be blue, and to miss him is dark grey. In the opening track, 'State of Grace', she admits she has often got it wrong, but now she is entering a golden age of hope. By *1989*, she was living in the kaleidoscope of New York City, but her relationship, as explored in 'Out of the Woods', was in screaming colour while the rest of the world was black and white. The Vault track 'Is It Over Now?' echoes the themes of 'Out of the Woods', with the red blood on white of the snowmobile accident where they lost control, and then the image of a girl in a blue dress, just like the paparazzi image of Taylor in the Caribbean after breaking up with Harry Styles. In 'Question?' from *Midnights*, he painted a colour she has searched for ever since. *Reputation* is loaded with references to blue eyes, and she promises she'll make his grey days clear. There are also shades of grey in the rebound relationship of 'Getaway Car', where the ties were black, the lies were white. Golden is the colour of the new, happy relationship – in 'Dancing with Our Hands Tied', her love had been frozen, but he painted her golden, and in 'Dress', she now has a golden tattoo of him on her skin.

This theme of blue and gold continued with *Lover* and into *Folklore* and *Evermore*. In 'Hoax', she doesn't want any other shade of blue but him, and in 'Coney Island', she asks if she painted his bluest skies the darkest grey. In 'Gold Rush', gold is the infatuation, as like Midas (who is also referenced in 'Champagne

Problems'), she dies for his touch. 'Invisible String' references an East Asian folktale about a red thread tying two soulmates together, and here it's a golden thread that pulled her out of the dive bar. It's the leaves on the trees as she journeyed from the green of their youth to this gold of heavenly love. Time gave her the blues and then purple-pink skies, but she is grateful for the pain of burning red love, as it brought her here.

In 'Ivy', the golden glow of an illicit relationship warms up her coldness, but with this warmth she's also playing with fire. 'Lavender Haze' is about a honeymoon relationship, and while the name was inspired by a '50's expression from *Mad Men*, there is also the ultraviolet light of 'Afterglow', which tells her the relationship she tried to sabotage is worth saving. Maroon is a more complicated, rusty colour than the burning red of how she saw love when she was young. By the time of 'Bejeweled', she cries sapphire tears, and in 'Hits Different', there are the catastrophic blues of the end of her relationship. 'The Great War' charts a relationship battle through colour, with bruising knuckles like violets (like 'Lavender Haze', given that haze is also mentioned). There is the crimson of blood all over the fields of clover, and once they are broken and blue, she calls off the troops. In 'So Long, London', she has held onto a relationship with a white-knuckle grip, where the lavender hope has faded. After entering the blue and grey of a dead relationship, she is finally getting colour back into her face. In 'Fresh Out the Slammer', she escapes from a relationship that was grey and blue. There is also a mention of greige in 'The Prophecy', an ambiguous, dull colour as she tries to work out what's going on in a relationship.

DRUGS Addictive, painful love is linked to drugs in songs like 'Florida!!!' It is also a dismissal of some of the shadier characters – in 'Vigilante Shit', it's implied he's doing lines of coke; in 'The Smallest Man Who Ever Lived', he tried to buy pills from a friend of friends; and he is stoned in 'The Tortured Poets Department'. She also mentions drugs in 'Don't Blame Me', where love made her crazy and he's like a drug that she will use for the rest of her life, and in 'Illicit Affairs', the high is like a drug that only worked the first few hundred times. In 'Who's Afraid of Little Old Me?' she acknowledges her narcotic references.

FAME Given her success, the poison chalice of fame is a common subject in her tracks. 'Castles Crumbling' is about being lauded and worshipped, but once the power goes to her head, she is now treated like a monster as they come for her. 'The Lucky One' tells the story of a young woman chasing fame, who goes from LA to the Riviera for the Cannes Film Festival, but as her secrets are splashed in newspapers, she just feels used. She is informed that there is a line of young things waiting to take her place, and as another name goes up in lights, she asks if she really is the lucky one. She chooses to disappear with her money and dignity, and to live anonymously rather than chasing fame. This is a familiar theme, too, in 'Nothing New' and 'Clara Bow', when she wonders what will happen when she is no longer the novelty and someone else lights up the room. In 'Karma', she asks what she has learned from her time in the spotlight, and why so many disappear when she is still here. 'Mirrorball' is about the shimmering, reflective side of fame, of trying to please as many people as possible, but it shatters and fragments. In 'Dear Reader', Swift leaves us with a reminder that she's a flawed role model, an unreliable narrator, and while they should look to another guiding light, she shines bright. She also reveals in 'Sweet Nothing' how she feels too soft for her industry of smooth talkers who make deals, and she prefers the safety of home. 'The Lakes' offers her an escape from those hunters with cell phones and the name-droppers who try to undermine her.

FLAMES The hurt at the end of a relationship is often equated to being destroyed by flames, with the symbolism first laid down in 'Picture to Burn' with the striking of a match. But flames are also a passion that can then be cruelly extinguished. He struck a match and then blew it out in 'Say Don't Go'. In 'Better than Revenge (Taylor's Version)', her love rival now holds the matches that lure him like a moth to the flame. In 'Style', she knows the relationship will burn up, but she can't bring herself to end it. In 'I Know Places', love is a fragile flame that could burn out. There is also flame symbolism in "'Getaway Car', and in 'Loml' they waltz back into rekindled flames, but he puts a match to their field of dreams. In 'The Black Dog', she's breathing clean air but she misses the smoke.

GHOSTS In '...Ready For It?' she wonders how many girls he has loved and left haunted. In 'My Tears Ricochet', the end of a relationship is like a funeral, and she didn't want to haunt him, but it's a ghostly scene. In 'Loml', they can't bury the relationship, and instead are killing time at the cemetery, but he's a ghost haunting her for telling her she's the love of his life and then running out. He promised rings and cradles, but they were dancing phantoms, and now she can't get out of bed. In 'Would've, Could've, Should've', she danced with the devil at 19 and now is scared of ghosts. The tomb won't close, as she is still filled with regret. In 'Anti-Hero', midnights become her afternoon as she stays up at night haunted by the people of her past that she ghosted. And in 'How Did It End?' the death rattle comes at the end of the dream, and instead of kissing, they sit like ghosts in a tree.

HISTORICAL FIGURES AND NOSTALGIA With a nostalgic, romantic eye for the past, Taylor has often found inspiration in the black and white photos of historical characters. In 'Timeless', she finds a box of old photos in an antiques shop, and the narrator imagines herself and her lover in these stories. 'Starlight' was written about Ethel Kennedy at the time when Taylor was dating Conor Kennedy. The track describes Ethel's romantic first meeting on the boardwalk in 1945, the yacht club party, and, like 'Mine', sitting by the water, dreaming of the future. 'The Last Great American Dynasty' is about Rebekah Harkness, the scandalous former owner of the house on Rhode Island, who Taylor compares herself to, as they both shock the town in their own ways and at different times. 'The

Bolter' was perhaps inspired by a similarly taboo-breaking woman, Lady Idina Sackville, who had a tendency to run away from her husbands, and who was a major character in Nancy Mitford's *The Pursuit of Love*. And then there are the tracks 'Epiphany' and 'Marjorie', which tell the stories of Taylor's grandparents.

LAWNS There are mentions of lawns in 'Mad Woman' and 'Vigilante Shit' as a form of trespass, and in 'Who's Afraid of Little Old Me?' she'll sue if you step on her lawn.

LITERATURE From some of her earliest tracks written when at school, Taylor has used literary references to cast a sentimental, poignant atmosphere, from *The Great Gatsby* to *Peter Pan* and *Alice in Wonderland*. 'Love Story' was a reimagining of *Romeo and Juliet* and the Capulet ball, and as she compares herself to a scarlet letter that Romeo has been warned to stay away from, it was as if she was being influenced directly by her high school readings.

In 'Wonderland', she's like Alice in Wonderland falling down a rabbit hole as a rushed relationship with a guy with a Cheshire Cat smile spins out of control. In 'Long Story Short', she fell from her pedestal right down the rabbit hole.

F. Scott Fitzgerald's *The Great Gatsby* is also a strong reference point. In 'This Is Why We Can't Have Nice Things', at Gatsby-style parties they jump into pools filled with champagne. This is similar to 'The 1', when, as she eulogizes the end of a relationship, she looks back on their Roaring Twenties to when they had something special. One of the most famous lines from *The Great Gatsby*, as uttered by Daisy, is also referenced in 'Happiness', when she hopes that her ex's new girlfriend will "be a beautiful fool", and she also looks to the green light of forgiveness, with green as the sign of hope for Gatsby as he stares out across the water to the green light on Daisy's pier. Taylor also confided to a *Vogue* reporter that one of her favourite quotes from a novel about Zelda Fitzgerald by Therese Anne Fowler was: "Look closer and you'll see something extraordinary, mystifying, something real and true. We have never been what we seemed."

Folklore and *Evermore* are rife with literary references, from Daphne Du Maurier's *Rebecca* as inspiration for 'Tolerate It', to the Peter Pan and Wendy namecheck in 'Cardigan'. He is the boy who can't grow up, and while he promises to come back to Wendy, she must move on from the foolishness of young love. This theme is also explored in 'Peter', from *The Tortured Poets Department*, as she sings to the lost fearless leader that she tried to be patient, but the girl who sat by the window had to turn off the light.

MADNESS In 'Champagne Problems', she would have made a lovely bride, they'll say, but she's fucked in the head. In 'This Is Me Trying', all her cages are mental. In 'Who's Afraid of Little Old Me?' she tells her listeners they wouldn't last an hour in the asylum where they raised her.

MANUSCRIPTS In 'The Story of Us', she declares the next chapters of a romance that turns to tragedy, while the love affair of 'All Too Well' was a masterpiece until he tore it up, leaving her like a crumpled piece of paper. In 'Holy Ground', the story's got dust on every page. In 'Suburban Legends', she hoped he would be more than a chapter in her diary, with the pages ripped out. They are a fresh page on the desk in 'Cornelia Street', and in 'Death by a Thousand Cuts', if the story is over, then why is she still writing the pages? This all culminates in the last track on *The Anthology*, 'The Manuscript'.

MIDNIGHTS Given an entire album was conceptualized around midnights, and that she created an *Evermore* sleepless nights edition, the middle of the night is a major theme in her works, right from one of her earliest songs, 'Teardrops on My Guitar'. She is kept awake at night by thoughts of her love, Drew, having found someone else. In 'Untouchable', again suffering from unrequited love, she dreams of him in the middle of the night, where the stars spell out his name. In 'Enchanted', she is still awake at 2 a.m. wondering if he loves someone else, and she conjures up an image of a sparkling, flawless evening that leaves her dancing around all alone at night, enchanted by the memories.

In 'Treacherous', headlights cut through the sleepless nights, and in 'All Too Well', she remembers kitchen dancing in the middle of the night in the glow from the refrigerator. She is awake at 4 a.m. in 'Better Man', as she tries to tell herself she was brave to run from this relationship. But it's in the middle of the night she misses him the most. In 'The Way I Loved You', she's up at 2 a.m., cursing him out because of the rollercoaster of her emotions due to insane love. And in 'Nothing New', she wakes in the night as she worries that she'll age out of the business at the age of 22.

She is also still awake at 3 a.m. in 'I Bet You Think about Me', as she imagines her ex fast asleep in his city with the perfect girl next to him. In 'Forever Winter', she tries to help a friend suffering from depression, but by 5 a.m. he's wasted and not listening to her.

Relationship regrets often come out in the middle of the night – in 'I Wish You Would', the narrator drives past her house at 2 a.m.; in 'Question...?' she asks if he had regrets of leaving in the middle of the night; and in 'The Last Great American Dynasty', she paces the rocks, staring out at the midnight sea. But it is also a time of fevered, passionate fantasy. In '...Ready For It?' the middle of the night is when she imagines what they would do together, and in 'Delicate', she's up at night with his hands in her hair. In 'New Year's Day', she wants his midnights, and in 'Paris', she imagines them escaping to Paris to see the tower lit up at night. In 'Daylight', the final track on *Lover*, she has awoken from a 20-year dark night, where in the morning light, everything is brighter.

MOVIES In 'Breathe', as she deals with the inevitability of a breakup, she imagines the music playing like the end of a sad movie. In 'Bye-Bye Baby', a *Fearless* Vault track, this time it wasn't like a movie and the rain didn't soak her clothes, and instead she drives away, lost in the grey. Given that she spent lockdown watching movies, the analogy pops up frequently in *Folklore* and *Evermore*. The character of Dorothea is a movie star in LA who sells dreams through the adverts in magazines. In 'The 1', she hits the Sunday matinee, and she says the greatest films of all time were never made. 'Exile', about coping with moving on from a relationship, offers a wry comment that they've seen the movie and didn't like the ending. In 'This Is Me Trying', she sees a flashback to a film reel that played on the one screen in her town. In 'Hoax', they know the hero dies at the end of the movie, so what's the point of making it? It's more romantic in 'Snow on the Beach', as a magical moment reminds her of one seen on the screen. But there is a bitterness to the cinephile in 'Loml', with all his plot twists and explosions.

PLACE Taylor's use of real-life places is catnip to fans as it's a means of gaining access to her world. From Cornelia Street in New York's west side to the Black Dog pub in London, they have become places of pilgrimage. Other places in Taylor's songs include Centennial Park in Nashville, mentioned in 'Invisible String' and where there is now a Taylor bench; Wicklow, Ireland, where Joe filmed *Conversations with Friends* and where they picked up a pebble in 'Sweet Nothing'; and all the London hot spots she namechecks in 'London Boy', including being a Tennessee Stella McCartney on the Heath. Although by the time of *Tortured Poets*, their home in Hampstead Heath had become a tomb of memories.

PLANES As well as a car crash, love is a plane crash. In 'Out of the Woods', they are paper airplanes flying, but then he hits the brakes too soon, ending up in stitches. In 'Labyrinth', she was sure the plane was going down, but somehow it turns around and has an exhilarating bounce back. In 'Getaway Car', they were jet-set Bonnie and Clyde, who were soaring at first, but then she has second thoughts and runs away.

PORCHES In 'We Were Happy', she remembers walking with him at night with the porch lights shining. In 'Fresh Out the Slammer', she is seeking solace from the end of a relationship with a past love who kept the porch light gleaming.

RAIN Throughout her albums, there has also been a common thread of rain – either the misery of being under rainclouds (the rain comes into her bedroom in 'Forever and Always') or the romantic passion of kissing in the rain, as in 'Hey Stephen'. In 'Fearless', she would dance in her best dress in a rainstorm because when he takes her by the hand, she feels fearless. In 'The Way I Loved You', she misses the screaming, fighting and kissing in the rain of a past relationship. In 'Sparks Fly', the way he moves is like a rainstorm, and she wants to be kissed in the pouring rain. He is like a ghost in 'How You Get the Girl', shaking from the rain when he apologizes for past mistakes. This is reminiscent of the earlier 'Come In with the Rain', where she leaves her window open at night in the hopes he'll come in. The rain washes away the pain in 'Clean', but in 'You All Over Me', a Vault track from *Fearless*, the rain has dried on the pavement, but she still feels him all over her.

ROOFTOPS In a very New York happening, she drinks beer and develops friendships and love on rooftops. In 'It's Nice to Have a Friend', they watch the sunset while playing a game of truth, and he touches her hand. In 'King of My Heart', her broken bones are mending as they spend time on the roof drinking beer in plastic cups.

SCARS Heartbreak is like a physical scar, an image first explored in her debut album's 'Cold as You' and 'A Perfectly Good Heart'. In 'Say Don't Go', she asks why he twisted the knife and left her bleeding and alone in the night. In 'Lover', she has the guitar string scar on her hand, in 'Willow', she asks to meet after dark to show the places others have given them scars, and in 'Cardigan', a comforting love drew a star around those scars.

SHADE The shade is both protective and restrictive. In 'Paris', she wants to sit quietly in the shade, away from the dazzle of celebrity, but in 'Fresh Out the Slammer', she equates being kept in the shade to a prison sentence.

SHIPS Their sinking is linked with the end of a relationship, or with the warning signs. In 'Dancing with Our Hands Tied', she wants to keep dancing as the water rushes in and the lights go out. In 'I Know Places', loose lips sink ships – she is running from the gossip that might destroy the relationship. 'This Love' offers a haunting promise of love like clear blue water rushing in, but then, as the skies grow darker, it disappears like a sinking ship. 'My Tears Ricochet' compares a fraught relationship to the battleships sinking beneath the waves. In 'So Long London', he tells her she abandoned their ship, but she feared she was going down with it.

SMALL TOWNS The small-town life has been a theme of Taylor's since her debut, where it is both innocent and stifling. Escaping the town for the big city is a theme in 'Mean', and she dreams of it while at high school in 'Fifteen'. In 'You're on Your Own, Kid', she dreams of getting out of the small town and the parking lot, the suburbia of sprinkler splashes. In 'Clara Bow', the starlet imagines swapping her small town for the dazzling lights of the city. In 'Midnight Rain', she left the small town that was like a cage to her, whereas he found it paradise.

STAR SIGNS Taylor has referenced astrology throughout her career and is said to be an expert in star signs. As a Sagittarius, her sign is the Archer, which earned its own track. In 'State of Grace', she mentions twin fire signs – Jake Gyllenhaal is also a December-born Sagittarius. There are mismatched star signs in 'Suburb Legends', which she hopes will surprise the doubters. In 'Mastermind', the planets, fates and stars all aligned to bring her to him.

SUBURBS The suburban life can be stifling. In 'Fortnight', she describes a suburban dream of backyards, neighbours and letter boxes, with a cheating husband she wants to kill. And in 'High Infidelity', in an unhappy relationship, his picket fence is as sharp as knives.

SUMMER This can be an optimistic, happy time, but it can also be the cruellest of confused emotions. The summer of youth went away in 'You're on Your Own, Kid', and 'The Smallest Man Who Ever Lived' ruined her sparkling summer. In 'Hits Different', summer felt like freedom on the coast after skipping town, but now the sun burns her heart now that it's over.

TOYS Destroying a toy signifies an immature person breaking what's around him. In 'My Boy Only Breaks His Favorite Toys', it was more painful because he took her out of the box to play with her, which left her with broken parts. She felt more with him than she did with the other "Kens", or identikit men, and in 'Hits Different', she used to ghost them. In 'Afterglow', she is the one who sabotages a relationship by breaking her favourite toy.

WAR In 'The Story of Us', she expresses a wish to shed her armour rather than fight. 'The Great War', depicts a relationship as a battle of bruised knuckles, and as in 'Afterglow', she's been poisoned by past experiences in wanting to punish him for things he never did. But when she sees him as a soldier on the icy ground looking truthful, she calls off the troops, and they plant a memory garden with vows not to start the war again.

WINE The heady taste of wine can be both intoxicating and depressing. In 'Dress', she spills wine in the bath, and in 'Maroon', not only do they drink cheap rosé, but he splashes it on her T-shirt. This links with 'Clean', where he's all over her like a wine-stained dress she can't wear anymore. She imagines, in 'Paris', that the cheap wine they drink is champagne, and in 'The Alchemy', she is hit by the dopamine of love, as if it's white wine. In 'The 1', the rosé is flowing, and it would have been sweet if she had been the chosen one to drink it with, and in 'Champagne Problems', the comfort and pleasure are wasted because she turned down a proposal. Now she finds solace in wine in 'Florida!!!' as *The Tortured Poets Department* reveals a dependency on alcohol to get through the end of a relationship. In 'Fortnight', as with 'Hits Different' and 'Dear Reader', she admits she was a functioning alcoholic who should have been locked away. In 'I Look In People's Windows', she is transfixed by the rose-golden glows of other people happily drinking wine with their friends.

ACKNOWLEDGEMENTS

As a long-time Swiftie who has found resonance in her poetic lyrics about love, loss and family, to write a book that charts Taylor Swift's journey has been a dream. I could play her music all day, so I didn't need an excuse to go back and listen to her albums one-by-one as I wrote and researched.

Thanks to Jo Rippon for commissioning me to write about Taylor, and to Claire Browne, Sarah Pyke and the team at Gemini for putting together such a beautiful book.

PICTURE CREDITS

Front cover: NBC-TV/Album/Alamy Stock Photo. Back cover: Kevin Mazur/Getty Images P4 Allen J. Schaben/Los Angeles Times via Getty P6 Kara Durrette /Getty P9 AP Photo/Mark Humphrey P10-11 Kevin Mazur/Getty P12 Jeffrey Ufberg/WireImage/Getty P13 TAS2023/Getty P14 Tony R. Phipps/FilmMagic/Getty P15 John Barrett/PHOTOlink/Alamy P16 Jason Merritt/FilmMagic/Getty P18 ZUMA Press, Inc./Alamy P20 ARCHIVIO GBB/Alamy P21 Jesse D. Garrabrant/NBAE via Getty P22 Rick Diamond/WireImage for CMT P23 Gardiner Anderson/Bauer-Griffin/GC Images P24L Christopher Polk/ACMA2010/Getty Images for ACMA P24R Michael Caulfield/WireImage/Getty P25 Michael Buckner/Getty P26 Shutterstock P28 Michael Buckner/Getty P30 Ethan Miller/Getty P32 Rick Diamond/WireImage/Getty P33 Kevin Winter/ACMA/Getty P34 Kevin Mazur/WireImage/Getty P35 Shutterstock P36 Associated Press/Alamy P37 Larry Busacca/Getty P38 Jason Kempin/Getty P39 Jason Kempin/Getty P40 Rodolfo Sassano/Alamy P42 Kevin Mazur/WireImage/Getty P44 AP Photo/Jason DeCrow P45 Sayre Berman/Alamy P46 Moviestore Collection Ltd/Alamy P47 Larry Busacca/Getty P48 Shutterstock P49 dpa picture alliance/Alamy P50 Kevin Mazur/WireImage/Getty P51 Devin Simmons/AdMedia/Sipa USA/Alamy P52 Andrew H. Walker/WireImage/Getty P54 PA Images/Alamy P56 James Devaney/GC Image/Getty P58 Kevin Mazur/TAS/Getty Images for TAS P59 Charles Sykes/Invision/AP P60(L) Alo Ceballos/GC Images (R) Alo Ceballos/GC Image (B) Jeff Kravitz/AMA2014/FilmMagic P63 Storms Media Group/Alamy P64 Barry Brecheisen/Invision/AP P65 Samir Hussein/Getty P66 Larry Busacca/MTV1415/Getty P67 (T) Dan MacMedan/WireImage/Getty P67 (B) Kevin Mazur/BMA2015/WireImage/Getty P68 Gareth Cattermole/TAS18/Getty Images for TAS P70 Shutterstock P72 Larry Busacca/Getty P73 (T) Alo Ceballos/GC Images P73 (B) Jackson Lee/GC Images P74 Joe Mahoney/Getty P75 Grzegorz Czapski/Alamy P76 Kevin Mazur/TAS18/Getty P77 Don Arnold/TAS18/Getty P78 John Shearer/TAS18/Getty P80 John Shearer/AMA2019/Getty P82 Kevin Mazur/Getty Images for iHeartMedia P84 (T) WENN Rights Ltd/Alamy P84 (B) Jeff Kravitz/2019 iHeartMedia P85 Kevin Winter/Getty Images for dcp P86 Rich Fury/Getty Images for iHeartMedia P88 John Shearer/Getty Images for 13 Management P89 Kevin Mazur/Getty Images for ABA P90 (T) Kevin Mazur/AMA2019/Getty Images for dcp P90 (B) Kevin Mazur/AMA2019/Getty P92 Kevin Mazur/AMA2019/Getty P94 TAS Rights Management 2021 via Getty P96 Theo Wargo/WireImage P99 Shutterstock P100 Shutterstock P101© Netflix / courtesy Everett Collection P102 Courtesy of MTV via Sipa USA/Getty P104 Daniele Venturelli/WireImage/Getty P105 (L) © Disney+ / Courtesy Everett Collection/Alamy P105 (R) AS Rights Management 2021 via Getty P107 ay L. Clendenin / Los Angeles Times via Getty P108 Kevin Mazur/Getty Images for The Recording Academy P110 Imago/Alamy P112 Kevin Mazur/Getty Images for The Rock and Roll Hall of Fame P113 Dimitrios Kambouris/Getty P114 Emma McIntyre/Getty Images for dcp P115 Rolf Vennenbernd/dpa/Alamy P117 Sarah Morris/FilmMagic/Getty P118 Kevin Mazur/Getty Images for iHeartRadio P119 Matt Winkelmeyer/Getty Images for dcp P121 Jeff Kravitz/Getty Images for MTV/Paramount Global P122 John Shearer/Getty Images for The Recording Academy P123 Shutterstock P124 Noam Galai/Getty Images for MTV P126 Kevin Winter/Getty Images for TAS Rights Management P128 Buda Mendes/TAS23/Getty Images for TAS Rights Management P130 John Shearer/Getty Images for TAS Rights Management P131 Kevin Mazur/Getty Images for TAS Rights Management P132 John Shearer/Getty Images for TAS Rights Management P133 AP Photo/Chris Pizzello P134 John Shearer/TAS23/Getty Images for TAS Rights Management P136 (T) Gotham/GC Images P136 (B) Johnny Nunez/Getty Images for The Recording Academy P137 John Angelillo/UPI/Alamy Live News P138 Jordan Strauss/Invision/AP P140 Kevin Mazur/Getty Images for The Recording Academy P142 Robert Kamau/GC Images P143 Gotham/GC Images P144 (T) AP Photo/Julio Cortez P144 (B) AP Photo/John Locher P145 AP Photo/Richard Vogel P146 Mike Coppola/Getty Images for MTV P147 TAS Rights Management/Getty P148 Bianca de Vilar/WireImage P151 Buda Mendes/TAS23/Getty Images for TAS Rights Management P152 Beth Garrabrant P153 Rodin Eckenroth/Getty P154 Kevin Mazur/TAS24/Getty Images for TAS Rights Management P156 Steve Russell/Toronto Star via Getty P159 Alishia Abodunde/Getty P160 Elyse Jankowski/Sipa USA/Alamy Live News P163 Xavier Collin/Image Press Agency/Alamy Live News P164 Robert Kamau/GC Images P 167 (L) Shutterstock P167 (R) Rick Diamond/Getty P167 (B) Larry Busacca/Getty P168 Isaac Brekken/Getty Images for Clear Channel P170 Kevin Mazur/WireImage/Getty P171 Kevin Mazur/WireImage/Getty P172 (TL) Taylor Hill/WireImage/Getty P172 (TR) Mark Davis/Getty P172 (BL) Dave J Hogan/Getty P172 (BR) Mat Hayward/GC Images P174 teve Granitz/WireImage/Getty P175 Christopher Polk/Variety via Getty P176 Kevin Mazur/WireImage/Getty P190–1 Neilson Barnard/Staff/Getty Images.